# LOCHNAGAR

## ALEX. INKSON McCONNOCHIE

With a new introduction by
Bryn Wayte, Deeside Books, Ballater.

Republished from the first edition of 1891.

This edition 2010.

DEESIDE BOOKS.com

Published by Deeside Books,
18-20 Bridge Street,
Ballater,
Aberdeenshire AB35 5QP
Tel. 01339 754080
Email: deesidebk@aol.com
Web: www.deesidebooks.com

ISBN: 978-1-907813-00-9


Printed and bound by Robertson Printers, Forfar

# INTRODUCTION

Little is known about the private life of Alexander Inkson McConnochie. Probably the most concise account of this author was given by Donald J. Withrington, Senior Lecturer in Scottish History at the University of Aberdeen, in his introduction to the James G. Bisset modern reprint of McConnochie's "Deeside", issued in 1985.

Withrington has gleaned information from such sources as the *Aberdeen Directory* to provide us with the knowledge that McConnochie was, by profession, an "accountant and law stationer". Born in Speyside in 1850, at Rothes in Morayshire, McConnochie seems to have spent the major part of his working life in the city of Aberdeen until moving to Glasgow in 1910, and then later to London where he died in 1936. It is during the Aberdeen period of his life that he produced the numerous guide books and pamphlets which proved to be extremely popular during the late Victorian period. This had been the time of the coming of the railways to many parts of the Scottish Highlands, which enabled relatively easy access to formerly remote areas. With this access hill walking became ever more popular, and there was now a demand for guide books, both for instructional and historical purposes. This was particularly true for the Deeside area, especially given the elevated status bestowed by royal patronage. The Aberdeen publishers were quick to grasp this and authors such as McConnochie were encouraged to write prolifically in order to capitalise on this new market. Hence the publication of "Lochnagar" in 1891.

McConnochie had an easily readable style of writing which portrayed the author's depth of knowledge both about his subject and about the area. There is no doubt that he was passionate in his feelings for the outdoors - to quote Withrington again 'A reviewer in the Scottish Mountaineering Club Journal (vol ii, January 1892) commented: Mr. McConnochie is a lover of nature and a hillman of the best type and most will agree with his dictum when he says "I hold that the true mountaineer is not the man who boasts of the number of peaks he has placed to his credit; the ideal hillman is one who thoroughly enjoys a day *on* the mountains, not hurrying and toiling up a Ben with the single purpose of rushing down again".' The latter part of this quote was taken directly from "Lochnagar", page 68.

McConnochie was one of the founder members of the Cairngorms Club and was the first secretary when the club was formally incorporated in 1889. When it was decided to publish a journal he became its editor as well, and contributed numerous articles himself over the years. This continued until his departure for Glasgow in 1910, which also coincided with the cessation of the publication of his books and pamphlets on the local area. Withrington attributes this to "possibly a sign that he had been driven along by the local publishers rather than an indication that he was running out of subject matter". His later publications in the 1920's were of a much more academic nature.

Speaking personally, and as a dealer in out of print books, I have always known that McConnochie's "Lochnagar" was a difficult book to obtain. It was frequently asked for, but, if available, only at a high price. I have no idea what the original print run was but few copies seemed to have survived with the original bindings. Those copies that did turn up always seemed to be ex-library copies with their own type of library binding. Fortunately, I was eventually able to obtain a copy in the original paper covered boards, which has been reproduced here in, hopefully, a more eye-catching version. Modern printing techniques now make it viable to reprint some of the older "classics" (copyright allowing). The merits of printing this book are two-fold. Firstly, it makes a scarce book more widely available and, secondly, if I make a profit it will help keep me in business.

Due consideration had been given to updating, revising and / or amending this first (and only) edition. But this was not the original reason for reprinting it, and I am sure that other people who are knowledgeable in the Gaelic language, local history and hillwalking will enjoy comparing the original with that which exists now. I have tried to be as faithful to the original as possible with only a few corrections to the text that were considered to be erroneous. Punctuation, wherever possible, was kept the same so as not to affect the style of writing, and all spelling, both English and Gaelic, are as McConnochie originally used. The original advertisments contained in the book are also included. I have always thought that, for any book, these show a "snapshot" of life at that time and can often give just as much information as that contained within the book itself, particularly for local historians.

A copy of the original one inch to one mile (1:63360 scale) map as incorporated by McConnochie is appended at the rear. However, this map is at times rather difficult to follow, both because of the amount of detail included and because of the mono colour (black). A magnifying glass is definitely needed. The nearest modern equivalent is the Ordnance Survey Landranger series 1:50,000 scale where the advent of modern printing techniques for the use of colour make the roads, rivers and contours much easier to differentiate. The area is covered in this series by numbers 43 and 44. However, by far the best maps available are the Ordnance Survey Explorer series, printed at the much larger scale of 1:25,000. These maps are sufficiently large to allow virtually all of the place names used by

McConnochie to be shown, and with just a few slight variations in the spellings used one hundred and twenty years ago there should be little difficulty in identification. The colour definition on these maps is superb, particularly for the contouring. The only slight problem is that McConnochie quotes heights in imperial but the modern maps are metric. Let common sense prevail and use the peak names for identification. Lochnagar itself is predominantly covered by number 388 in this series whereas the Braemar portion falls on the adjoining numbers of 387 and 404. A brief mention should also be made about river delineations here - McConnochie adopted the convention of always facing downstream when describing the left or right river bank.

For further reading on the Upper Deeside and Lochnagar areas the following books still in print may be recommended:

Ian Cameron. Plant & Roots: A Social History of Ballater.
Ian Murray. In the Shadow of Lochnagar and also The Dee from the Far Cairngorms.
Dr. Sheila Sedgwick. The Story of Ballater and also numerous others about Deeside.
Adam Watson. Scottish Mountaineering Club District Guide - The Cairngorms.

For a specific history of the "mounths" and the passages over them Robert Smith's "Grampian Ways" is probably the best available, first published in 1980 and last reprinted in 2002. The standard historical reference work for Deeside is probably taken to be "The Royal Valley" by Fenton Wyness published in 1968. Further advice will be freely given for other books of local interest.

Finally, it is hoped that the reader will enjoy this book for the purpose that it was originally written - to describe the walks around and on Lochnagar along with a brief history of the area.

Bryn Wayte,
Deeside Books,
Ballater,
June 2010
www.deesidebooks.com

# LOCHNAGAR

D·WYLLIE AND SON

C·D·WYLLIE

EDWD YOUNG

·ABERDEEN·

# LOCHNAGAR

BY

## ALEX. INKSON M<sup>C</sup>CONNOCHIE

AUTHOR OF "BEN MUICH DHUI AND HIS NEIGHBOURS: A GUIDE
TO THE CAIRNGORM MOUNTAINS"; "BENNACHIE"; &C.

ABERDEEN

D. WYLLIE & SON

1891

TAYLOR AND HENDERSON
LITHOGRAPHERS AND PRINTERS TO HER MAJESTY
ADELPHI PRESS, ABERDEEN

TO

**Alexander Cruickshank LL.D.**

IN GRATEFUL ACKNOWLEDGEMENT

OF

KINDLY ASSISTANCE FREELY RENDERED

**By the same Author.**

BEN MUICH DHUI AND HIS NEIGHBOURS: A guide to the Cairngorm Mountains. *With Map.* Boards, 1/-

BENNACHIE: Its Topgraphy, Historical, Traditional and Ballad Lore, Geology and Botany. *With Map and Illustrations.* Boards 1/-; Cloth 2/-

LOCHNAGAR: Its Topography, History, Traditions, Geology and Botany. *With Map and Illustrations.* Boards 1/-; Cloth, 2/-

*In preparation.*

(Uniform with BENNACHIE and LOCHNAGAR.)

DEESIDE: From Aberdeen to the Wells of Dee. *With Maps and Illustrations.* Boards 1/-; Cloth 2/-

# CONTENTS

MAP

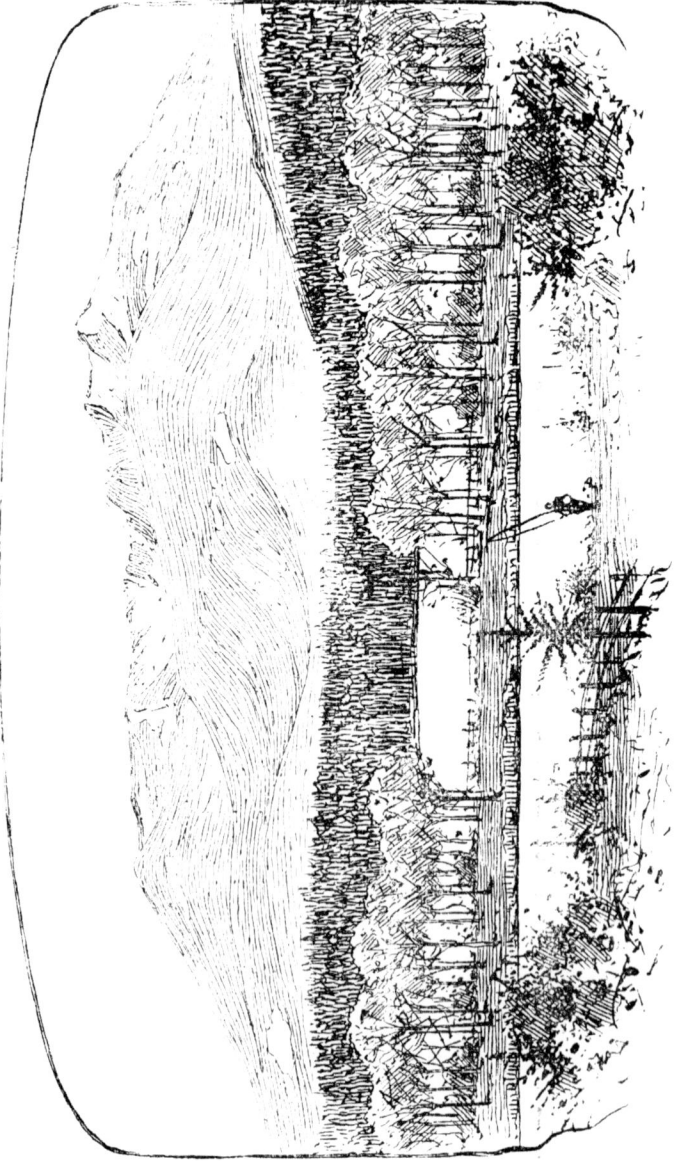

LOCHNAGAR.

# LOCHNAGAR.

## CHAPTER I.

## THE WHITE MOUNTH.

*When ye White Mounth frae snaw is clear,*
*Ye day o' doom is drawin' near.*

F ROM many localities in the North-East of the central division of Scotland, especially in the County of Aberdeen and in the valley of the river Dee, a high mountain attracts the eye, from its majestic aspect, its precipices, and its culminating ridge and peak. This mountain, popularly called Lochnagar, but more correctly the White Mounth, is situated on the South side of the Dee in its upper part - some 45 miles inland from the North Sea - and forms the highest point in a mountain range which was long known among the high lands of Scotland by the name of the Mounth, and more recently as part of a larger range called the Grampians. The mountain range of the Mounth may be deemed to extend along the South side of the Dee upwards of 60 miles in a direction W.S.W. from the sea at the Girdleness (a little south of Aberdeen), along the conterminous borders of the County of Aberdeen on the North, and the Counties of Kincardine, Forfar and Perth on the South, to Carn an Fhidleir, at the South-West corner

of the County of Aberdeen, near the head or North
end of Glen Tilt. Here the Mounth abuts at a right
angle on a great mountain range called the Dorsum
Britanniae or Drum Alban, which forms part of the
ridge or backbone of Scotland, and acts as the watershed of the Tay and Forth, and part of the West
boundary of Perthshire.

Mr. Skene, however, in his *Celtic Scotland* says:-

"The Mounth extends in nearly a straight line across the
island from the Eastern Sea, near Aberdeen, to the Western
Sea at Fort-William, having in its centre and at its western termination the two highest mountains in Great Britain - Ben
Muich Dhui and Ben Nevis . . . . If the Mounth is *now*
known as the range of hills which separates the more southern
Counties of Kincardine, Forfar, and Perth, from those of Aberdeen and Inverness on the north, it was not less known to the
Venerable Bede, in the eighth century, as the steep and rugged
mountains which separate the provinces of the southern from
those of the northern Picts".

While about a dozen of British mountains reach a
higher altitude than Lochnagar, it yet holds a distinctive place alike in fact and in fancy. It has much to
offer to the student, the lover of nature, and even to
the ordinary sight-seer - more than many of its nomin-
al superiors. In the popular mind Lochnagar has
had adventitious aids to its prominence. One who
afterwards became a great poet lived under its shadows
when he was young, and became so impressed with its
wild crags and its frowning glories, that in after years
he sang of them in undying strains - strains that have
spread its name and its fame through all lands. Then
for more than forty years, one who has been even
greater as a Queen than Byron was great as a poet,
has delighted to dwell at its base, and has often

climbed to its summit. Thus Lochnagar has attained special distinction for itself, and through those who have been associated with it; and one may therefore be pardoned who seeks to take up the story of the mountain, and to tell, as best he can, of its configuration and its features, its peaks and its precipices, its corries and its lochs, its surroundings in glen and river, its legends and traditions as they still linger (though ever growing more indistinct) in the memories of those who have their homes within its influence. The writer hopes that he may be able to present an interesting and in some degree instructive account of the mountain which, more than any other, ever comes before the mind as essentially and characteristically Scottish, and yet having associations that seem to make it the common property of every man, woman and child, throughout the world, who has any aquaintance with English literature and history.

The term "Mounth" is of considerable antiquity. Wyntoun, in his *Orygynall Cronykil of Scotland* - a work written in verse in the beginning of the fifteenth century - speaking of Macbeth, says :-

> O'er the Mounth they chased him there,
> Intil the Wood of Lumphanan.

There is also a proverbial saying, "He's over the Mounth", which points to the general use of the name in olden times. Popularly, however, the term Mounth has fallen out of use in favour of the term Grampians, which has been applied loosely to the mountain systems of the central Highlands of Scotland. Hector Boece in 1521 adopted the name Grampians from the term Mons Grampius or Granpius, applied by Tacitus to the place where Agricola and the Romans in A.D. 55 defeated Galgacus and the Caledonians, and Skene supposes this place to have been near the junction of the Tay with the Isla. This may have led to the popular application of a fine euphonic term like that of "the Grampians" to an extended range of hills, as Home makes his hero do in the tragedy of "Douglas" :-

My name is Norval. On the Grampian hills
My father feeds his flocks.

Notwithstanding the disuse of the term "the Mounth", enough remains, in some cases slightly disguised, to show its general application to the range which forms the watershed between the North-flowing tributaries of the Dee, and the South-flowing streams of the Tilt, Shee, Isla, South Esk, North Esk and Bervie Water. Beginning at the East end of the chain, we have on the South side of the Dee, not far from Aberdeen, "Causey Mounth", in the Parish of Banchory-Devenick and County of Kincardine, on the road which formerly led from the South, through Sir Walter Scott's "Muir of Drumthwacket", to the ferry of the Dee and so to Aberdeen. This ferry was, a little above the railway bridge over the Dee at Aberdeen, at what is still known as the "Foords of Dee", which ferry was rendered unnecessary by the erection of the Bridge of Dee, begun by Bishop Elphinstone in 1500 and completed in 1516 by Bishop Gavin Dunbar. In the year 1380 Paul Crabb, tenant of the lands of Kincorth, on the South side of the ferry, gave an annuity towards the support of the "Causey Mounth" road, so called from the line of road passing through a moss which required causeying to render it passable. From this circumstance the name of the farm, "Causeyport", on the edge of the moss can be understood. Next we have "Slug Mounth", from Stonehaven by the West side of Cairn Mon-earn to the Dee; and then the "Cairn-o'-Mounth", on the borders of the parishes of Fordoun and Strachan - the latter one of the principal roads between the South and the North. Still further Westward there is the "Fir-Mounth" - so called from the abundance of trees in the olden time where it intersects Glen Tanner - or, as it is sometimes simply called, the "Mounth" or "Mount" Road. This was the ancient public road between Brechin and Ballater, crossing Mount Keen, which latter hill was often known as "Mounth Keen". The word is next met with in "Capel Mounth" - the name of the much-frequented (in olden times) pass between Glen Clova in Forfarshire and Glen Muick in Aberdeenshire. Then we have the "White Mounth" (Lochnagar), and to the West of it is "Tolmount", on the borders of the Counties of Forfar and Aberdeen at the watershed of Glen Doll and Glen Callater - Doll being probably a corruption of Toll. This last "passage" has become more widely known from the recent unsuccessful attempt of the new proprietor of Glen Doll to shut up the ancient right-of-way.

The old names, thus specified, mark the ancient paths across "the Mounth" which in former times were in constant use. The introduction of good roads and railways into the Highlands rendered the most of these paths and drove roads of little use for their original purposes. The drover may yet be seen at intervals on these ways; the tramp is still to be found on most of them; and the tourist has also to be reckoned with. In fact, the pedestrian tourist has shown himself determined to maintain the rights acquired from his predecessors, and he will doubtless tenaciously keep his grip of the keys of the picturesque, if not commercial, roads of his native country.

The meaning of the word "Month, Mounth", is thus given in Jamieson's Scottish Dictionary:- "1, a mountain;   2, the Grampian mountains towards their Eastern extremity". He derives the word from the Anglo-Saxon *monte*, doubtless the same as the Latin *mons*, *montis*, a mountain. Another authority ascribes the term "Mounth" to a peculiar kind of mountain grass.

In the Ordnance Survey maps the name "White Mounts" will be found on the high table-land between the two little lochs Lochnagar and Dubh Loch, the word "mounts" being obviously a mistake for "mounth". The Rev. George Skene Keith, D.D., in the appendix to his *Agricultural Survey of Aberdeenshire*, published in 1811, says of Lochnagar, that "the second top, or border of the White Mounth" was 3780 feet in height. The inference from these and the other facts stated is plain - that the old name of the mountain, now universally known as Lochnagar, was "the White Mounth". As it is the highest point in "the Mounth" the title was peculiarly appropriate, because then as now, snow would naturally lie longest on it.

Lochnagar is the highest mountain on the South side of the river Dee. It is situated in the great Highland district of Mar, in the County of Aberdeen, and is drained solely by tributaries of the Dee. The highest point is in the united Parish of Crathie-Braemar, but the greater part of the table-land of the mountain lies in another united Parish, that of Glenmuick-Tullich-Glengairn. The Northern portion of the mountain is mostly in Crathie, the Southern in Glenmuick; and it will be convenient hereafter to refer to these united Parishes as Crathie and Glenmuick respectively.

There are, as already mentioned, a few higher mountains in Scotland than Lochnagar, but none more generally or deservedly popular. The beauty and grandeur of the mountain itself are amply sufficient to render Lochnagar of the utmost interest to the mountaineer and the lover of nature. It sufficiently overtops and stands apart from its surrounding compeers to give dignity to its appearance when seen either from the vicinity or from a distance; its corries are deep and numerous; its precipices perpendicular and "frowning"; it abounds in lochs in most picturesque positions; and its general outline, especially as seen from the East and North, is most graceful. It is readily recognisable from most of the chief hills of Aberdeenshire, and from many lower parts in the same County, as well as from hills in other Counties; and, to crown all, the prospect from its summit is barely surpassed by that from any of our inland mountains of even greater altitude. The lover of mountain scenery, the geologist, and especially the botanist, will find Lochnagar of peculiar interest. Further, it may be mentioned that while all the valley of the Dee is deservedly famous for its scenery, Upper Deeside, in which Lochnagar is situated, is specially thus distinguished, and is noteworthy also from antiquarian and historical points of view. Braemar Castle, Invercauld House, Balmoral

Castle, Abergeldie Castle, and other buildings (or ruins) of
general interest are at the very foot of the mountain,
and with other attractions render the ground classic.

The boundaries of Lochnagar are well defined by
natural depressions containing lochs and streams. On the
North there is the river Dee; on the East its tributary the Muick, with Loch Muick; on the South
its chief environments are Loch Muick, Dubh Loch,
and Loch Callater; and on the West are the Callater
Burn and the Clunie Water, the latter another great
tributary of the Dee, entering it near Braemar Castle.
The extent of Lochnagar as thus defined is considerable.
The distance between the mouths of the Muick and
the Clunie is about 13$^{1}/_{2}$ miles, while from Dubh Loch
to the Dee at Balmoral is 7$^{1}/_{2}$ miles. But the mountainous mass of Lochnagar may be more correctly estimated by taking the distance between the Muick and
the Callater Burn (by the South side of Lochnagar) as
9 miles, and from Dubh Loch to a point 1250 feet in
height near Balmoral Castle on the Gelder Burn as
nearly 7 miles, giving altogether an extent of about 63
square miles of country, elevated more than 1250 feet
above the sea level. At the same time it must not be
forgotten that "the Coyles" between the Muick and
the Girnock, and Craig Choinnich, in the lower angle
of the Dee and the Clunie - to which reference will
again be made - must be considered as stepping-stones
to Lochnagar, seeing that at only one point does the
height of the intervening ground sink slightly below
1250 feet.

Lochnagar, on a little consideration, will be found
to be a strange and unique name for a mountain, even
in this the land of mountains, where nice differences

in the appellations of heights are carried out to an extent that only the Gaelic language appears to admit. As applied to the mountain the term "Lochnagar" is a misnomer, that name only belonging properly to the small loch that lies at the bottom of the crags near the highest point of the White Mounth (Cac Carn Beag). An old native of the district, when questioned as to the absolute accuracy of the expression "on the top of Lochnagar", replied, "You could only possibly be 'on the top of *Loch*nagar' in a boat or during very frosty weather"! I am not aware of any other instance of a mountain bearing the name of a loch without the prefix of the word "Ben" or something similar, so as to distinguish loch from mountain. Nor have I been able to trace when the name of the loch was transferred to the mountain, but the change must be comparatively modern. Lord Byron, however, has sung of it as "Lochnagar", and so doubtless it will remain to the end of time.

The meaning of the word "Lochnagar" has provoked not a little discussion, even the spelling not having been generally agreed on at one time. As for the latter, a reference may be permitted to Blaeu's map (of 1654), where the loch is marked as "L. na Garr", the mountain itself being there nameless. I am inclined to think that "Lochnagar" signifies "the loch of the goat", the mountains in this neighbourhood, as in many other parts of the Highlands, abounding at one time with goats. Indeed the name "Gar" occurs several times in the vicinity, the nearest instance being "Creag nan Gabhar" a little to the West of Loch Callater. "Creagan nan Gabhar" is also the name of a small craig between Glen Dee and Glen Luibeg,

while "Lochan nan Gabhar" is the name of a lochlet
on the North side of Ben Avon. The highest point
of the Beinn a' Ghlo group of mountains in Glen Tilt
is known as "Carn nan Gabhar". (The letters *bh* in
these examples are mute.) But the Rev. Alexander
Stewart, LL.D., better known to many as "Nether Lochaber", an authority on Gaelic topography, holds that
"Lochnagar signifies Loch na *gaoir* or Loch na *gair* -
the loch of the *sobbing and wailing* when the mountain
winds sweep across its expanse. The mountain ought
clearly to be called not Loch-na-gar but Ben-na-Gair".
Mr. Donald Mackinnon, M.A., Professor of Celtic Lan-
guages in the University of Edinburgh, thus writes me
on the subject:- "With all the aids available many of
our Gaelic names are as yet unexplainable. I would
not myself hazard even a guess as to the meaning of
the *gar* in Lochnagar without obtaining, first, all the
old forms that can be got, and, second, the exact
pronunciation by the people of the district. With
such help the vocable may remain still obscure; without it any suggested derivation must remain at best a
guess more or less happy, but of no scientific value.
The language has undergone great change, and the
place-names frequently preserve the most reliable
evidence we, in Scotland, in the absence of many
written documents, possess".

There are no less than eleven summits on Lochnagar, each with a height of upwards of 3,000 feet above
the sea level. These summits are :-

|   |   | Height in feet. |
|---|---|---|
| 1. | Cac Carn Beag, ... ... ... | 3786·2 |
| 2. | Cac Carn Mor, ... ... ... ... | 3768·1 |
| 3. | Carn a' Choire Bhoidheach, ... | 3630 |

Height in feet.

4. Cairn of Corbreach,       ... ... ... 3571
5. Cuidhe Crom,            ... ... ... ... 3552·4
6. Creag a' Ghlas-uillt,      ... ... ... 3450
7. Carn an t-Sagairt Mor,   ... ... ... 3429·6
8. Carn an t-Sagairt Beag,    ... ... 3424
9. Meikle Pap,             ... ... ... ... 3210·8
10. Little Pap,             ... ... ... ...
11. Meall Coire na Saobhaidhe,    ... 3190·5

(The "summits" numbered 3, 4, 6, 8, and 11, do not require attention from the general tourist.)

Cac Carn Beag, a natural "cairn", stands between Lochnagar (the loch) and Lochan an Eoin, but nearer the former. It slopes on the North towards Meall Coire na Saobhaidhe, from which it is distant, there being a depression between them, about seven furlongs.

Cac Carn Mor is a quarter of a mile to the South-South-East of Cac Carn Beag, and close to the top of the rocks at the bottom of which is "Lochnagar". The cairn is partly artificial.

Cairn of Corbreach is immediately above, and on the South side of, Lochan an Eoin; there is no "cairn". Carn a' Choire Bhoidheach is a little to the South of it, lying between Allt a' Choire Bhoidheach on the East, and Allt na Da Chraobh Bheath on the West - the two most northerly head streams of the Muick. It is unmarked by a cairn: Creag a' Ghlas-uillt, also unmarked, lies to the South-East of Carn a' Choire Bhoidheach, between the Glas Allt and Allt an Lochan Buidhe, two burns flowing parallel.

Cuidhe Crom, which faces the mountaineer as the ascent is made from Glen Muick, lies to the West of

the head streams of the Allt na Guibhsaich and Northward from the Glas Allt. It is marked "3552" on the
one-inch O. S. map. The Meikle Pap is to the North
of it, at a distance of about three quarters of a mile,
while the Little Pap is to the South, at a distance of
about a quarter of a mile - these three summits being
almost in line. The two "Paps" are readily recognisable from their shape, these modern names being simply
translations    from    the    Gaelic    "Ciche    Mhor"
and "Ciche Beag" respectively.

Carn an t-Sagairt Mor, marked "3430" on the
one-inch O. S. map, is between Loch Callater and
Lochan an Eoin. It is better known as Meikle Cairn
Taggart - or simply Cairn Taggart. A ridge of it to
the Westward of Lochan an Eoin is called Carn an
t-Sagairt Beag, or Little Cairn Taggart.

Cac Carn Beag, Meall Coire na Saobhaidhe, and
Meikle Pap are in the Parish of Crathie; Carn a'
Choire Bhoidheach, Creag a' Ghlas-uillt, Cuidhe Crom,
and Little Pap are in Glenmuick; while Cac Carn
Mor, Cairn of Corbreach, Carn an t-Sagairt Mor and
Carn an t-Sagairt Beag are on the border of these two
Parishes.

Besides these eleven summits there is a large
number of minor peaks that need not be referred to
here. Exception ought perhaps to be made as regards
Conachcraig, a range of about four miles in length on
the East side of Glen Gelder, which attains an altitude of
2827 feet. Several of the lower summits along the
Dee are familiar to the public, from the memorial
cairns erected on them by the Queen.

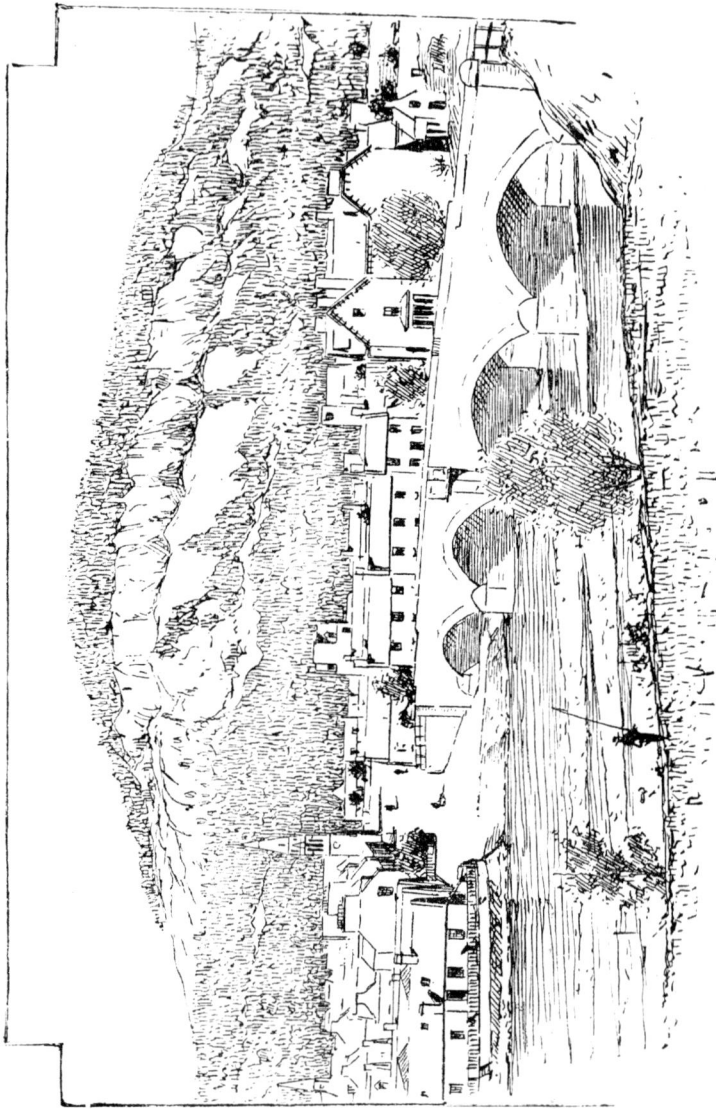

BALLATER.

# CHAPTER II.

# BALLATER TO LOCHNAGAR.

Donjons, and towers, and castles grey
Stand guardians by the winding way.

## I. Ballater to Alltnaguibhsaich Lodge, via Spital

THE principal points from which Lochnagar is approached and ascended are Ballater and Braemar. All other routes are of comparatively little importance, but will be duly referred to in the course of the work. From Ballater the distance to the highest summit of the mountain is 13¹/₂ miles, but of that 9 may be driven, leaving only 4¹/₂ for walking. The village of Ballater is 43¹/₂ miles by rail and 42 by road from Aberdeen, and stands at a height of 658 feet above sea level, on the left or North bank of the Dee, in the Parish of Glenmuick. Claiming to be the capital of the Deeside Highlands, it is nevertheless of modern, not to say of recent date. Ballater, as a Highland summer and autumn resort, has a popularity second to none in the North, but till 1760 the site of the village was a bare moor, without a single house - Tullich, some two miles down the river on the same side, having then the Church, Inn, Post Office, &c., although it is now all but deserted. In 1760 the Wells of Pannanich, about two miles below Ballater on the South side of the Dee, became famous as a health resort. The hamlet of Pannanich and the village of Ballater were accordingly built for the accommodation of the seekers after health    and pleasure who flocked to "The Wells". According to the *Edinburgh New Philosophical Journal* of 1830, Ballater is "always crowded - during the summer months with invalids and other visitors, brought together by the fame of the chalybeate wells of Pannanich and the magnificence and beauty of the surrounding scenery". The Wells have greatly declined in public favour; but Ballater has steadily increased in size and popularity - having even attained the dignity of a police burgh - and is still growing rapidly. G. Fenwell Robson in his *Scenery of the Grampian Mountains*, a fine work published in 1814, gives several capital views of Lochnagar, one of which is taken from the vicinity of Ballater. In that view the village appears to consist of the Church and about half-a-dozen houses, at the base of that gigantic mound of rock, Craigendarroch, which dominates it on the North side.

Starting from Ballater to Lochnagar the Dee is crossed by a handsome granite bridge, and the South Deeside Road - to the right - is taken. This bridge was opened by the Queen only a few years ago, and is the fourth that has been constructed almost at the same point within the past hundred years, and already it is being spoken of as not likely to have a long life. A direction post at the South end of the bridge gives the following information :-

| Pannanich, | 1³/₄ Miles. | Glenmuick [House] 1 | Mile. |
|---|---|---|---|
| Dinnet Bridge | 6¹/₂ " | Abergeldie | 6¹/₄ " |
| Aboyne | 11 " | Balmoral | 8¹/₂ " |

The ruins of Braichlie Castle and the modern Braichlie House are passed a little to the left, and

fully half a mile from Ballater Bridge the Bridge of
Muick is reached, near where the Muick joins the
Dee. Here the traveller has the option of two ways
up Glen Muick towards Lochnagar - one by crossing the
Muick and going up what is known as the Balmoral
side from the property there belonging to Her Majesty;
the other by keeping the right bank of the Muick and
going along the road on the Mackenzie side, so called
from that portion of the glen belonging to Sir Allan
Mackenzie of Glenmuick. It will be more convenient
to deal with the latter route first.

Leaving Bridge of Muick behind, a handsome
Episcopal Church is soon passed a little to the left,
and a short distance beyond it stands Glenmuick
House; while Birkhall, the property of the Queen,
may be seen a little farther away on the opposite side
of the Muick. About half a mile above Birkhall is
Mill of Sterin, to which a cart road leads down from the
right. To the pedestrian who is anxious, to avail
himself of the shortest route, it is advantageous, to cross
the Muick here, but meantime it is assumed that the
Mackenzie side is kept. The next point of interest is
the Falls of Muick, which, however, are more conveniently seen from the Balmoral side. Emerging from
the wood above the Falls the bare and higher
portion of the Glen is entered, though from the old
tree roots that are met with in the upper parts, it is
evident that it had at one time been wooded throughout, and had afforded capital shelter for the wild swine
that presumably had formerly abounded in the Glen -
for Glen Muick signifies the "sow's valley". It may
be noted how well watered this side of the glen is,
affording capital grazing for deer. The streams on this

side of the Muick rise, in the lower part of the glen, on the watershed of Glen Tanner, and in the upper on that of Glen Mark.

At this point a good view of Lochnagar, or rather of some of its summits, is obtained. On the left the Little Pap may be readily recognised, and to the right of it Cuidhe Crom and Conachcraig - the two latter as though there were no gap between them. The Conach-craig range is apt at first blush to be mistaken by strangers as forming the main mass of Lochnagar. But by the time a ford across the Muick is passed (known as the Ford of Inschnabobart), such a mag-nificent view is got, that there is no mistaking the monarch of the Mounth. Passing the Ford, to which a rough cart-track on the right shows the way, there are, also on the right, the ruins of an old public-house known as "Teetabootie" (look about you). These ruins are recognisable by the circumstance that several houses had been in line and close to each other. Three quarters of a mile farther up the Glen is Spital of Muick, the end of our driving road on this side. Spital of Muick is now represented by a gamekeeper's house, with, on the opposite side of the road from it, the ruins of a public-house, which (in 1815) succeeded Teetabootie. At the back of the keeper's house is a "Loupin'-on Stane", where the last "landlady" was wont to mount her pony. From this stone a footpath, rather indistinct in some places, leads over the Muick (by a foot-bridge at a height of 1298 feet) to Alltna-guibhsaich Lodge, about three quarters of a mile distant. The Lodge, which is surrounded by trees, cannot be mistaken, there being no other house in the neighbourhood.

A halt may now be made before commencing the ascent, and during the rest a brief account may be given of the more interesting features of the route that has been traversed. Braichlie Castle was among the first of these mentioned. Its ruins are scanty enough now, for they have been "vandalised", the stones having been carried off to serve in the erection of more modern buildings. The place is popular from the well-known ballad entitled "The Barrone of Braichlie", of which the first two lines are :-

> Inverey came down Deeside whistlin' and playin',
> He was at brave Braichlie's yetts ere it was dawin.'

The ballad tells of a successful attack made on 7th September, 1666, by Farquharson of Inverey on Gordon of Braichlie, a relation of the Earl of Huntly. The old avenue approach, lined with ash trees, may still be seen from the road, the entrance to Braichlie House being a little beyond. The property of Braichlie, as well as the whole of the South-East side of Glen Muick, was purchased in 1863 from the late Colonel Farquharson of Invercauld, by the late Sir (then Mr.) James T. Mackenzie, the proprietor of Kintail. The Farquharsons purchased Glen Muick some time during the seventeenth century from the Gordons, by whose then head, the first Earl of Huntly, it had been acquired. Mr. Mackenzie entertained the Shah of Persia at Glenmuick House, during a portion of his visit to Deeside in 1889, and at the beginning of 1890 he was created Baronet of "Glen Muick". The Episcopal Church here was built by him in 1875, and his remains, as well as those of several members of his family, are interred in a large vault near the Church, which is dedicated to St. Nathalan, the patron saint of the old Parish of Tullich. (The ruins of Tullich Church may be seen as Ballater is neared from the East. There is a curious story that the famous Reel of Tullich was composed and first danced at this Church on a cold winter Sunday in the "olden time".) A short distance above St. Nathalan Church is Glen-muick House, erected by Sir James T. Mackenzie in 1873. It occupies a commanding position, and appears to advantage from Ballater. The ground plan sur-rounds three sides of a quadrangle, and the structure has basement, ground, first and attic floors. The public rooms are very handsome. The whole building is lighted by gas made near by.    The North, which is the principal elevation, has a handsome portico, with a covered-in   carriage way, surmounted by a massive-looking square tower 75 feet in height. The building is of granite, large blocks of stone having been obtained in the neighbourhood, without much quarrying. It is in the Tudor style of architecture, so treated as to harmonise with the surrounding scenery.

A little above the wood, beyond the Falls of Muick, Allt an t-Sneachda (the snowy burn, doubtless well named) joins the Muick, and is crossed by a wooden bridge, on the South side of which is a cairn, said to mark "where the last wolf was killed in Scotland". But other places also claim that distinction. It is very probable that the cairn simply marks the spot where a funeral party had rested, it having been very common thus to indicate these places.

The Inschnabobart Ford is very old, having existed before there was a road on the left bank of the Muick. It was then mostly used in connection with the road

GLENMUICK HOUSE.

leading from the Dee at Easter Balmoral, by the upper part of Strath Girnock, to the Muick at Inschnabobart, and so on to the South by the Capel Mounth. After the road on the left bank of the Muick was made, a foot-bridge was thrown over the stream, but it was taken down in 1863. It would be a great convenience to the public were it replaced, as it would allow of a considerable saving being effected in the walking distance, by enabling pedestrians to cross the river here, instead of their requiring to make a detour by Spital Bridge. Previous to 1836 the driving road on the right bank of the Muick stopped short at the Inschnabobart Ford.

Nearing Spital a view of the highest point of Loch-nagar is obtainable. Here, as at most other points, he is pleasing and grand, devoid of that lumpishness which distinguishes most of the higher Cairngorm mountains. On the left there is Little Pap, then Cuidhe Crom and Meikle Pap, with, between the latter two, the crags that form "the steep frowning glories of dark Lochnagar". Behind these crags is to be seen the peak of Cac Carn Beag. The Meikle Pap will be recognised by the deep square cut on its rocky top; to the right of it, a deep hollow intervening, is Conachcraig, which is to the North-East of Lochnagar. The Muick, heretofore very bouldery, now winds smoothly and slowly along through mossy ground, with "peat-banks" on its sides, while remains of old shielings are plentiful,

The inn or public-house at Spital of Muick - like its predecessor at Teetabootie - stood on one of the old roads from the North to the South. This particular road crossed the Capel Mounth, between Forfarshire and Aberdeenshire (as mentioned in the first chapter), and from Spital it turned down Glen Muick to the valley of the Dee. "Spitals", it may be mentioned, were planted in almost all the mountain passes of Scotland, as well as in other places, being occupied by Churchmen, and managed in pretty much the same manner as the famous Hospice of St. Bernard on the Alps. At a very early date the Muick Spital was established by the Bishop and Chapter of Aberdeen. It stood on Allt Darrarie (the noisy burn), a tributary of the Muick, which rises in Coire Gorm where Aberdeenshire appears to enter, tooth-like, into Forfarshire. This Spital was well placed, and doubtless many a wayfarer was indebted to the Churchmen for providing that accommodation and "refreshment for man and beast" which otherwise it would have been difficult to obtain in such a locality. It is also evident that this and other Spitals served as side-chapels for the population which existed where they were planted, or that grew up around them. It need not be told here how the Churchmen and the Spitals were separated. A public-house was conducted at Teetabootie till 1815, when the fall in prices, resulting upon the declaration of peace after the Bonaparte wars, brought disaster to the tenant and to other residenters in Glen Muick, as it did to so many stock-dealers and farmers elsewhere. From Teetabootie the business was transferred to the Spital, where it was continued till 1846. Only a small portion of the gable of the public-house - which was understood to  be close to the site of the ancient hospice - now remains. The Allt Darrarie formerly flowed close past the house, but, as it was apt to cause damage when in flood, it was diverted, about 1837, to some little distance on the East side. The old channel is quite dry now, but perfectly distinct; and, spite of the bulwark made to change the course of the stream, a considerable spate would send its waters down by the old bed. One is very apt in mist to lose the Capel Mounth path, when proceeding *from* the South Esk, the track by the Capel Burn being indistinct in several places. Many have, as a consequence, wandered down the Allt Darrarie, a longer and rougher route; and several have lost their lives in storms in the upper part of that glen. About three miles above Spital a rough stone, on the left bank of the Darrarie, marks the burial place of "Couper" Glass. He was last seen at Spital, and it was not for several months after his death that his body was found. Foul play was suspected by some as the cause of death, but most probably he died from exposure, aimlessly walking into Forfarshire after a carouse in Glen Muick. Some distance above Glass's grave a mound may be seen, below which are the remains of a man and a lad - likely father and son. They were found dead during a sheep-gathering, both having died from the effects of a severe storm which had overtaken them as they were entering Aberdeenshire by the Capel Mounth. They were believed to be umbrella-menders from the contents of a pack found beside their bodies.

It is difficult now to realise the great numbers of cattle and sheep that formerly passed Spital of Muick, on their way from the extreme North to the South of Scotland, and even into England. All cattle were so driven at one time, and the glen routes were preferred alike on account of their softness for the animals' feet (which were sometimes shod for the journey), and

because of the feeding by the way. This, the Capel
Mounth route, was a popular pass, and Spital public-
house a favourite and convenient halting-place, as cattle
often rested here for two or three days. Crowds of
Highland shearers, men and women from the North,
travelled yearly on foot by this route, to assist in har-
vesting the crops in the South. In going and returning
they spent the nights in barns and outhouses, often
making merry, a piper generally accompanying large
parties to supply music for a dance. Naturally enough
high words would sometimes on such occasions arise
among the drovers and shepherds; and a cairn, still
standing, points out the spot where, between Spital and
the Muick, after one of these merry-makings, a shepherd
was found dead with marks on his body testifying that
death had resulted from foul usage. The shepherd's
name was Donald Gordon, and his body was found the
following morning by two women on their way South
with a "birn" of stockings. It is yet related how "the
landlord" led his family and servants to the body,
making each lay his hand on the dead man's breast to
prove his guilt or innocence. According to the well
known old superstition, if a murdered man was touched
by any person who had participated in the slaughter,
the guilt of that person would be declared by the spurt-
ing of blood from the wounds or the mouth of the
corpse. Another cairn about a mile South from Spital
by the pass road, marks the spot where a shepherd
named Stewart perished in the snow, in 1843. Farther
along is the "Pack Merchant's" Cairn - showing where
a "Packman" was murdered for the contents of his
purse, which were believed to be considerable. Another
cairn - "the Souter's" - was   raised to commemorate

the finding of the body of a shoemaker who, towards the end of last century, got the reputation of occasionally informing on the smugglers. He met his death on the Capel Mounth, by being allowed to take his fill of spirits from a party conveying their smuggled goods to the South. This party left him behind, drunk, and, falling asleep, he died from exposure.

By 1846 the formation of better roads in the low country, and the making of railways, had almost abolished the traffic upon such drove roads as that passing through Glen Muick and over the Capel Mounth, and so the public-house disappeared, as the Churchmen's hospice had done. Perhaps the public-house might still have found a number of customers, but deer forests and grouse moors were coming into fashion, and it is stated that "the laird" thought the old hostelry was becoming a resort for poachers, and, accordingly, he helped it out of existence. In this neighbourhood there is now but the one solitary "reekin" lum, the gamekeeper's, to be seen, but the number of "larachs" (ruins) scattered along the river side, including those of a schoolhouse near Teetabootie, indicates that in former days a considerable population must have earned their livelihood in the district. Indeed the rigs of what was once cultivated land are still quite distinguishable. There are also remains of a corn kiln and a meal mill, while the ruins of a smuggling bothy show that here, as in other Lochnagar glens, there had been manufacture and trading now deemed illicit.

## CHAPTER II. - (Continued)

## BALLATER TO LOCHNAGAR.

*2, Ballater to Alltnaguibhsaich Lodge, via Bridge of Muick*

O ! the Hi'elands are bonnie, when the heather's in bloom,
An' ilk strath, where you wander, smells sweet wi' perfume.

BRIDGE of Muick is about three-quarters of a mile South-West of Ballater, and carries the South Deeside turnpike over the stream, near the point where it falls into the Dee. A direction post at the bridge gives the following distances:-

| | | |
|---|---|---|
| Falls of Muick, | ... ... ... | 5 Miles |
| Loch Muick, | ... ... ... | 8$^{1}/_{2}$ " |
| Birkhall, | ... ... ... | 1$^{3}/_{4}$ " |
| Balmoral, | ... ... ... | 7$^{3}/_{4}$ " |

Crossing the Bridge the traveller to Lochnagar is upon the Balmoral side of the Muick, the road on which is better, but rather longer, than on the Mackenzie side. On the left-hand side of the road at the West end of the Bridge of Muick is the churchyard of the old Parish of Glenmuick, and the manse of the united Parish may be noticed on the opposite side of the road. Half-a-mile beyond, on the left, is a standing stone known as "Scurry Stane". The farm here is named after the stone, and so was a Roman Catholic Chapel which stood in its immediate neighbourhood. A short distance beyond Scurry Stane the Glen road, trending South-West-wards, leaves the turnpike at a point

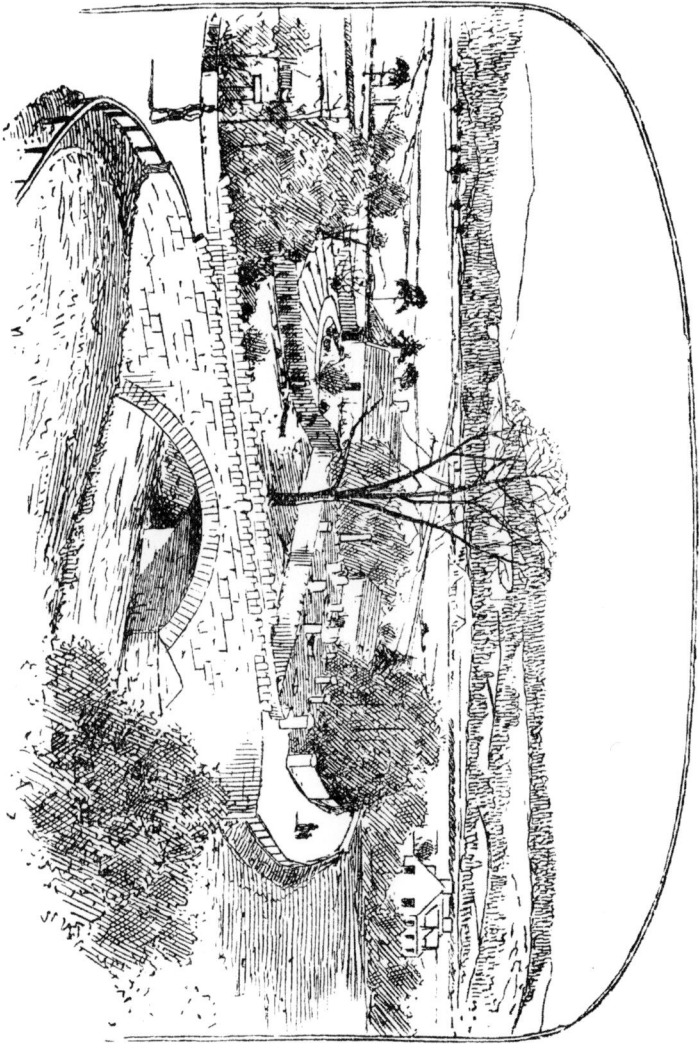

BRIDGE OF MUICK.

near the foot of a hillock or "cnoc" on which are the ruins of Knock Castle, and the Royal property of Birkhall is passed on the left, about a mile farther on. Half-a-mile beyond Birkhall may be seen, on the left, Mill of Sterin (the clattering mill), where there is a wooden bridge, with stone piers, over the Muick. Between Mill of Sterin and the Falls of Muick stand the miniature mountains named the Coyles of Muick. The Falls are surrounded by the Linn Wood, and are consequently heard before they are seen. After the wood is left behind, the Muick, with its peaty banks, shows but a poor contrast to the brattling river it was in the lower portion of the Glen. Beyond the Falls is Inschnabobart (the field of the poet's cow), a small farm having its steading on a brae on the right. Being about 1300 feet above the sea level, this farm has the highest cultivated land in the Glen, and the farm house is the only dwelling between the Falls of Muick and Alltnaguibhsaich Lodge, which is about a mile and a half distant in a Southerly direction.

The present Bridge of Muick was built in 1878, replacing one which had stood on the same site for 140 years, and which had the usual high-centred arched roadway that marked the bridges of former times, and enabled travellers to know "when they were on them and when they were off them".

The old Church of Glenmuick stood in the churchyard, on the left-hand side of the road, imme-diately to the West of the bridge. In pre-Reformation days it was dedicated to the Virgin Mary. It would appear to have been a very poor building in the last century, for the writer of the Statistical Account in 1794 says that the Church then was "a very old house

thatched with heath". In 1798 a new Church was
built in Ballater (on the site of the present Parish
Church), and, strangely enough, on the night the found-
ation of that Church was laid, the old building at
Bridge of Muick was burned. According to one
account, the minister's wife had hen nests *inside* the
Church, and the maid, looking for eggs with a lighted
bit of fir, accidentally set fire to the edifice. Another
account has it, that the Church was burned intention-
ally, with the view of destroying certain records concerning the Farquharsons of Invercauld, which that
family were not particularly anxious to have preserved.
These records are said to have been compiled by
Priests of Scurry Stane Chapel, and to have been
handed by their successors to the minister of Glenmuick. That story, although it still lingers in the
district, is rather wanting in probability, because Roman
Catholics carefully preserved and retained for themselves all their old records, and there is no hint that
any of the Farquharsons or their friends, had a hand in
the fire. Not a vestige of the ruins of the old Church
is now to be seen. The burial place of the Gordons
of Abergeldie is in the churchyard, distinguished by a
high obelisk, within an iron railing. An exceedingly
interesting tombstone stands close to the entrance gate
of the churchyard. It is a rough coffin-shaped granite
slab having the following inscription very rudely cut
upon it:-

1596

I.M :

1722

The initials are said to be those of John Mitchell, who
lived at Dalliefour, in Glenmuick, about a mile to the

KNOCK CASTLE.

North-West of the churchyard, and the dates are believed in the locality to be the years of his birth and death respectively! Tradition asserts that Mitchell was a skilful angler and a famous poacher.

The Parish of Glenmuick, according to the earliest authorities, belonged to the Earl of Mar, his successors being respectively the Earl of Crawford and the Earl of Huntly. The grant to the latter is dated 29th January, 1449-50. In the course of time the land passed from the Earl of Huntly, head of the Gordons, to some of the younger branches of the clan, and latterly the Abergeldie estate alone remained to the Gordons.

Knock Castle (so named from its site) is a grey picturesque ruin, and is so sheltered and enclosed with trees as not to be readily discernible from the road. The Castle replaced a tower which had stood for centuries near the same site, and which dated back to the times of the ancient Earls of Mar. It would appear to have been held, along with the lands of Glen Muick, early in the fourteenth century, by a family named Bisset, and to have passed in succession to the Frasers, the Keiths (Earls Marischal), and the Gordons (Earls of Huntly). At one time the Castle was held by the Durwards, and was garrisoned with the view of maintaining the Royal authority on Upper Deeside. Alexander the last Gordon of Knock, is believed to have built the present Castle. According to tradition his line ended in a single day. A feud having existed between him and "Black" Arthur Forbes of Strath Girnock, a "broken man", the latter fell upon Gordon's seven sons while they were casting turf, and killed them all before any resistance could be made, sticking their heads on their "flauchter-spades". When the news was carried to Gordon of Knock he fell down dead. His kinsman, Gordon of Abergeldie, having the power of "pot and gallows" from his Chief the Earl of Huntly, made a summary end of "Black" Arthur. He then seized the lands of Strath Gimock, to which he served himself heir, while the lands of Knock fell to him by inheritance. Latterly they were included in the Birkhall portion of the Abergeldie estate.

Birkhall was formerly called Sterin, which name is still in use at the mill above. It formed part of the Abergeldie estate till its purchase for the Prince of Wales, from whom Her Majesty acquired it a few years ago. Birkhall, although only a plain three-story house, is a delightful residence, surrounded by trees of various descriptions. The original front, which is ivy-clad, faces the Muick, but an addition, of the same height, looks towards Ballater. Above the front door is the inscription :-17. CG.RG. 15.

Mill of Sterin was formerly a meal mill, but after 1838, when the glen began to get depopulated, meal mills became little needed, and the water power was utilised for a sawmill, which is still in operation. Another meal mill stood at Aucholzie, further up the Muick. The road above Mill of Sterin is private, so far as public carriages are concerned, but under certain conditions it may at times be used as far as Alltna-guibhsaich Lodge. Sometimes, when driving on the Mackenzie side, the Muick can be forded at Inschna-bobart, instead of driving up to Spital - the part of the road on the Balmoral side *above* Inschnabobart being held by some to be public.

BIRKHALL.

The Coyles of Muick are prominent objects from Ballater, as well as from many other points. The name is derived from Coille a wood or forest. *The* Coyle attains a height of 1956 feet, and is surmounted by a big cairn. The following inscription is carved upon a stone which is meanwhile lying at the foot of the cairn :-

ERECTED

BY COMMAND OF

QUEEN VICTORIA

IN REMEMBRANCE OF

THE MARRIAGE OF

ALBERT EDWARD PRINCE OF WALES

AND

ALEXANDRA PRINCESS OF DENMARK

10TH MARCH 1863

When the marriage of the Prince of Wales took place, the tenants on the Birkhall estate built a commemorative cairn on Creag Bheag, one of the minor Coyles (the one nearest the Muick), but as that cairn became ruinous Her Majesty caused the present one to be raised on the higher point. The elements, however, have not paid much respect to this cairn. The green tops of the Coyles are due to the scantiness of the heather on them. *The* Coyle consists of serpentine, a soft rock the soil from the decomposition of which is inimical to the growth of heather. The serpentine continues for nearly two miles towards the North in several bare peaks, and to it succeeds hornblende slate, mica slate, and porphyry.

"The Laird's Bed", a bit of sloping rock, may still

be seen on *the* Coyle. Here the Laird of Birkhall found occasion to betake himself for a time after the '45. Meall Dubh (the black lumpy hill), another of the Coyles, composed of hornblende slate, once possessed a slate quarry, and the roof-covering for Birkhall House was obtained from it. Eagles are at times yet to be seen on the Coyles; no less than six were seen together on a certain occasion "hunting" a wounded hare.

On the West side of the Coyles two fir trees standing close together may still be seen, which, according to popular belief, have a history of their own. It seems that several centuries ago there had been three trees on this spot, one of them having been cut down by the younger of two brothers who had the grazing on the Coyles. The elder brother had objected to the tree being felled, and even cursed the trees themselves, and every person that dared lift an axe on them. Nevertheless, his brother having cut down the tree, built a barn with it; but the barn was soon burnt to the ground. Shortly after the tree-feller got into financial difficulties, and ultimately died a drivelling idiot - all following, it was generally held, upon his brother's curse! The malediction also has been strong enough to preserve the other two trees to the present day; and woe betide the man daring enough to touch them!

At the Falls of Muick the glen is contracted and richly wooded (larch trees predominating), and the banks of the stream are profusely adorned with wild flowers and ferns in the summer and autumn months. The Falls are thirty to forty feet in height, descending over hornblende slate, some parts of which are laminated and intersected by granite. Her. Majesty often pays them a visit during her residence at Balmoral. When snow is lying thickly in the vicinity, and the rocks are covered with ice, the Falls have a peculiar beauty that, to many eyes, transcends their summer charms. Despite many an effort, salmon are unable to ascend the Falls; but a salmon ladder would remedy that. Were such a ladder constructed there would be a slight loss to the picturesque, but the fish would be enabled to take advantage of the fine ground for spawning beds in the river above the Falls, and also to reach Loch Muick. According to Pennant the "hole" of the Falls was "supposed by the vulgar to be bottomless" - a belief entertained in regard to almost every pool that could not be readily plumbed by the simplest methods at command in bygone days. Like the gorge at the Linn of Dee, the Muick is so contracted that it can be stepped over in dry seasons at the point where the water commences its plunge down the rock. Above the Falls the water seems to be forming cavities in the rock of more or less circular shape. On a recent visit the writer examined a cavity, the depth of which proved to be 14 inches after a quantity of pebbles had been removed from it. At the surface of the rock its diameter was about 4 inches, and it was sufficiently wide to allow the hand to get easily to the bottom. One striking peculiarity is that the water could only have acted while the Muick was in spate upon the rock in which this cavity is formed.

Beyond the Falls, the great hollow containing Loch Muick presents itself to view. It appears girt about with mountains, having steep fronts with flattish

summits. The effect produced under certain atmospheric conditions, with play of sun and mist, is weird
and fanciful.

A small burn (now known as Allt a' Mhaide - the
Fox's Burn) joins the Muick at Inschnabobart, close
to the West end of the Ford, and is crossed by a neat
stone bridge. The old name of this streamlet signified
"the burn of the two sticks", referring doubtless to the
fact that it had formerly been crossed by a bridge con-
sisting only of two trees laid lengthwise. The first cart
with wheels in use at Inschnabobart was brought there
in the first decade of the present century from Kirrie-
muir, having been drawn over the Capel Mounth by
two horses, with four men rendering assistance.

The Allt na Guibhsaich (the fir tree burn) flows at
the back of the Lodge (or Shiel, as it is sometimes
called). The road crosses it by a neat wooden bridge
with stone piers, at which public carriages have to stop.
The present bridge, as well as the road, was made by
the Queen, and replaced a bridge and road made by
the Gordons of Abergeldie, the new road being named
the "Prince's Drive". The "Gordon" road, and one
that had preceded it, can still be traced - the piers of
the old bridge being about forty yards above the new.
But the old route to Lochnagar did not cross
the burn, the path, which can hardly now be traced,
leading up the left bank of the stream. The Lodge
was formerly called "The Hut", and it really
deserved that name in the end of the last century, when the roof was covered with sods and the
house had but one "lum". In 1810, however, the
Rev, Dr. Skene Keith, speaks of it as "a most com-
modious cottage belonging to Captain Gordon" of

Abergeldie. Writing in 1850 the Rev. Mr. Grierson says:- "It is called 'The Hut', and consists of three rooms, and a kitchen detached". Now it is a neat little "Lodge" with two public rooms and about half a dozen bedrooms. It is a most charming occasional residence about a mile North of the foot of Loch Muick, which is visible from the front of the house, a number of trees having been cut down to admit of the view. The Queen and the late Prince Consort frequently spent a night or two at the Lodge. The ruins of humbler abodes may be seen in the neighbourhood, showing that this side of the Muick, as well as the other in the neighbourhood of the Spital, had formerly a considerable number of inhabitants, where now, under the new order of things, a single household would find difficulty in subsisting.

## CHAPTER II. - *(Continued)*

## BALLATER TO LOCHNAGAR.

*3. Alltnaguibhsaich Lodge to the Dubh Loch.*

Lands may be fair ayont the sea,
But Hielan' hills and lochs for me.

HAVING reached Alltnaguibhsaich Lodge from Ballater up Glen Muick, the mountaineer is at the real starting point for the ascent of Lochnagar. A capital excursion may, however, be occasionally made from the Lodge to Loch Muick, the Glasallt Shiel, the Falls of the Glasallt, and the Dubh Loch, by a route which, while in some parts solitary and grand, is of the most picturesque character throughout. There is a driving road from Alltnaguibhsaich Lodge to the Glasallt Shiel near the head of Loch Muick, a distance of about three miles, and a pony path leads from the Shiel to the Dubh Loch. These places are all on Her Majesty's estate, and the roads have been specially made at the Queen's expense. Even were that not the case, no one would think of intruding on the Queen's privacy, and one can easily ascertain when the Queen is at Balmoral. Previous to the purchase of Balmoral by Prince Albert a rough path led along the North-West side of Loch Muick, but the ancient track - which may still be traced in several places - was much improved upon by the Queen. It was by this old route that cattle were formerly sent to graze on Lochnagar for a few weeks during summer. The

Queen does not, like many landowners, threaten the pains of law for trespass, but boards bearing the words "Strictly Private" are exhibited at the starting points on the roads which have been specially formed at Her Majesty's cost. A written permission must be obtained before carriages may be driven beyond the entrance gate of Alltnaguibhsaich Lodge.

The summit of Lochnagar may be ascended from the Dubh Loch, but there is no path. The route is by the main stream of the burn which flows into the Loch, and which, near its sources, is crossed by a well-defined path - the route from Loch Callater to Cac Carn Mor.

The distance from Alltnaguibhsaich Lodge to the lower end of Loch Muick is about a mile. The Loch lies at an altitude above sea level of 1310 feet, and is fully two miles in length, by about half-a-mile in breadth, covering an area of 960 acres, with a depth in many places of over 60 fathoms. The general direction of the Loch is South-West to North-East. It has a small islet at the upper end, on which sea-gulls formerly bred. Cormorant, teal, and mallard have been shot over it, and the gosander has been repeatedly seen. Even the wild swan is not altogether unknown; some twenty years ago one tarried a week in the vicinity and was spared by the keepers, but was shot when it went lower down the Muick. When on the banks of the Loch one is struck by its solitude and grandeur, so much is it enclosed by mountains. Still the Loch is by no means dreary, for its banks are sufficiently fringed with trees to lighten up the cheerless and gloomy aspect which often characterises sheets of water in the Highlands, when they are so grasped

around by hills as Loch Muick is. The mountain
ridge on its South-East side culminates in Black Hill,
which attains a height of 2470 feet. At the bottom of
this hill is a capital path along the Loch side from Spital
of Muick to the head of the Loch. This path proceeds in such a well-defined straight line that it detracts
somewhat from the picturesque appearance of the
Loch when viewed from its left bank. The track,
which was recently made, is a continuation of the
driving road on that side of the glen, which, as a
public road, ends at Spital of Muick. It is, however,
continued on for nearly a mile to Lochend, at the
lower end of the Loch. Here there is an insignificant
shooting-box, with a boat-house, and here the foot-path
just mentioned begins. Fully half-way up the Loch
this path crosses the Black Burn which enters the
Loch at a sandy beach, the only spot on that side
which is free of boulders. Between it and the head of
the Loch the hilly ground is known as the Fir Roads,
from the fact that at one time the natives of Clova
were in the habit of coming here for trees for roofing
purposes. Concerning the nature of the ground on
this side, it is interesting to refer to the Rev. Thomas
Grierson, author of *Autumnal Rambles among the
Scottish Mountains* (1851), who says that "there is not
the slightest vestige of its ever having been trod by a
human foot"; and that the edge of the Loch would
not "admit of anything like safe progress, however
slow". The mountain, he says, is "so abrupt to the
very brink of the Lake that the large loose stones are
often dislodged, thus endangering the limbs and life
of the pedestrian". The result of Mr. Grierson's
wanderings in this vicinity (he had    been    taking a

glimpse of the Dubh Loch), was a night in the open air, and as, doubtless, many mountaineers are doomed to such experiences in the course of their explorations, let us see how the reverend gentleman passed the night. "After collecting some heath and spreading it on the sheltered side of a rock I composed myself for rest, having put on dry shoes and stockings, and made myself as comfortable as circumstances would admit. I confess I felt not a little dreary at first, especially as I had neither meat nor drink of any description in my fishing basket. Most fortunately, I had a thick short greatcoat, which I had worn all day, much to my annoyance, but which was now my chief comfort. Fagging on under this had caused a profuse perspiration, so that, as soon as I had relaxed my labours, I became as cold as if I had been cased in ice. Gradually, however, I grew tolerably warm, and passed seven hours and a-half far more agreeably than I had reason to expect. Though *without food*, I could yet ruminate, and I even enjoyed some refreshing sleep. The noise of numerous cascades from the sides of Lochnagar, directly opposite, served as an agreeable lullaby, forcibly reminding me of the graphic, admirable description of our great national bard-

> 'Foamin' strong, wi' hasty stens,
> 'Fraclin to lin;'

When day dawned, I was not a little astonished to see the upper half of Lochnagar white with snow, which had descended on me in slight showers of rain". In the morning our belated brother-mountaineer duly reached Spital, where "the porridge-pot was soon suspended over a splendid peat fire, both of which

I was right glad to superintend after my recent fast and bivouac". The inn, however, which was expected to be found here, had been shut for several years.

Loch Muick is a favourite spot of the Queen's and is frequently referred to in her *Leaves from the Journal of our Life in the Highlands*. In writing of a row up the Loch the Queen says:- "Here we found a large boat, into which we all got . . . . They rowed up to the head of the Loch, to where the Muick runs down out of the Dubh Loch . . . . The scenery is beautiful here, so wild and grand - real severe Highland scenery, with trees in the hollow. We had various scrambles in and out of the boat and along the shore, and saw three hawks, and caught seventy trout. I wish an artist could have been there to sketch the scene; it was so picturesque - the boat, the net, and the people in their kilts in the water and on the shore". In another chapter the Queen says of the South-East side of the Loch that it "is very fine indeed, and deeply furrowed by the torrents, which form glens and corries where birch and alder trees grow close to the water's edge. We landed on a sandy spot below a fine glen, through which flows the Black Burn. It was very dry here; but still very picturesque, with alder-trees and mountain-ash in full fruit overhanging it. The moon rose, and was beautifully reflected on the Lake, which, with its steep green hills, looked lovely. To add to the beauty, poetry, and wildness of the scene, Coutts played in the boat; the men, who row very quickly and well now, giving an occasional shout when he played a reel. It reminded me of Sir Walter Scott's lines in *The Lady of the Lake* :-

'Ever, as on they bore, more loud
And louder rung the pibroch proud.
At first the sound, by distance tame,
Mellow'd along the waters came,
And, lingering long by cape and bay,
Wail'd every harsher note away'.

We were home at a little past seven [having left Alltnaguibhsaich Lodge at half-past four], and it was so still and pretty as we entered the wood, and saw the light flickering from our humble little abode [Alltnaguibhsaich Lodge]".

In the walk along the side of Loch Muick, Alltan Dearg (little red burn) is crossed. It is a pretty little stream rising on An t-Sron and the Monelpie Moss (jagged moss) and falls into the Loch about a mile from the point at which the river Muick runs out of it. An t-Sron (the nose) is the culminating point of the steep ridge on the left bank of the Loch, and attains an altitude of 2326 feet. The Alltan Dearg derives its name from the red granite through which it has cut its way down the face of the mountain. The cleft thus formed in the rock is very deep and extensive, quite beyond, one would think, the power of such a streamlet. The cutting becomes very conspicuous as one proceeds along the Loch side, and in its deepest recess is a pretty waterfall which was formerly much visited by the Queen, but the pony path leading up to it is now neglected and overgrown. The "Braes of Glasallt", as the South-Western ridge of An t-Sron is sometimes called, are immediately to the South-West of Alltan Dearg. Writing in 1852 Her Majesty says:- "We arrived at the Alltan Dearg, a small burn and fall, which is very fine and rapid. Up this a winding

path has been made, upon which we rode; though
some parts are rather steep for riding. The burn falls
over red granite; and in the ravine grow birch,
mountain-ash, and alder".

The Glasallt Shiel stands near the upper end of
Loch Muick, on the right bank of the Glas Allt (grey
burn) at its confluence with the Loch. This Shiel is
the most remote of Her Majesty's Lochnagar residences,
and, while unpretentious, is a very neat - it may be
said pretty - building of two stories, now surrounded
by firs, planted mostly since the Shiel was built. It
would be difficult to find a house with a more pleasant,
and, at the same time, retired situation; it is quite
unique of its kind. Above the front door, which faces
the Loch, is the inscription :-

VICTORIA REGINA.
1868.

What might be taken for an old horse-shoe is affixed
to the door of one of the outhouses; but it is understood that this token of good luck fell from one of the
mules that rendered service in the Egyptian campaign.
Several of these animals were purchased by Her
Majesty after the battle of Tel-el-Kebir, and a few of
them were taken to Balmoral and used as deer ponies
on Lochnagar. Two or three steps from the door of
the Shiel is a miniature harbour for a boat to row over
the Loch. So genial is summer here that, in a bit of
garden ground behind the Shiel, potato "shaws" have
in recent years attained a height of six feet, while in
the vicinity heather may be found growing to a height
of six feet six inches, and "dockens" to no less than
seven feet! This is the sunny side of the picture at

GLASALLT SHIEL.

the Glasallt Shiel; but what about it in winter? Then pebbles larger than pigeons' eggs are blown over the top of the house, and the ice on the Loch has measured twenty-one inches in thickness even in March! The front windows of the house occasionally come to grief from wind and stones. The Shiel almost occupies the site of an old shooting-box of the Gordons of Abergeldie, and at the back of it may still be traced the foundations of a shepherd's hut which had existed in the olden time. The Prince Consort had long wished to build a "Shiel" at the Glas Allt, this neighbourhood having been a great favourite of his; so after his death the Queen erected the present building. The "house warming" was on 1st October, 1868, and, in describing it, Her Majesty tells that she felt it essential to have a new house in the district, as she could not have lived alone at Alltnaguibhsaich Lodge, where she had spent so many happy days with the Prince.

The Glas Allt rises almost at the very summit of Lochnagar, less than half-a-mile to the South of Cac Carn Mor. The burn has two head streams, the space between which is known as the "Tongue of the Glas Allt" - a name precisely descriptive of the rounded ridge indicated. The larger of the two head streams runs through Coire an Daimh Mhoile (corrie of the "hummel" stags). This corrie was so named at the desire of the Prince Consort, who here shot two stags without horns. About half-a-mile above the junction of the Glas Allt with Loch Muick the burn has a very fine waterfall over granite rocks, known as the Falls of the Glas Allt, which are well worthy of a visit. They are about 150 feet in height, and are situated within a little rocky corrie which forms about three-fourths of a circle. The rock is reddish in some parts, but "glas" (grey or dun) is a correct description of the prevailing colour. Within the corrie is nothing but rock and grass, and not much of the latter. A pony path, very steep and very zig-zag, leads up to the Falls from the Shiel. The Queen thus writes of the scene:- "We walked on [from Alltan Dearg] until we reached the higher part of the Glas Allt, which we stepped across    .    .    .    Then we began the descent of the Glas Allt.  .  .  . From here it is quite beautiful, so wild and grand. The Falls are equal to those of the Bruar at Blair, and are 150 feet in height, the whole height to the foot of the Loch being 500 feet. [The latter height has now been ascertained to be about 660 feet.] It looked very picturesque to see the ponies and Highlanders winding along. We came down to the Shiel of the Glasallt, lately built, where there is a charming room for us, commanding a most lovely view". The path from Balmoral Castle to Glasallt Shiel, by Glen Gelder and Monelpie Moss, crosses the Glas Allt just above the Falls.

Creag na Sithinn (the craig of fairy knolls) which attains a height of 2312 feet, is a short distance to the South-West of the Falls of the Glas Allt, and is well worth ascending from them. From the summit a capital view may be obtained, especially of Loch Muick, which seems to lie at one's feet. Creag na Sithinn is surmounted by a "watcher's" shelter, but the elements have been too much for the roof. Nearly a mile to the West of Creag na Sithinn is a small lochlet, named Lochan Buidhe, about 300 yards by 70 in extent. It is thoroughly embosomed among mountains - one could scarcely fancy a more retired position for a sheet of water. Allt an Lochan Buidhe, which rises between Creag a' Ghlas-uillt (the craig of the Glas Allt) and Creag an Dubh-Loch (the craig of the dark loch), flows through it, entering the Lochan at a point almost mid-way in its length, and leaves exactly opposite the entrance, thus using the *sides* instead of the ends as is generally the case. The inlet is smooth and rocky; the outlet is not unlike that of Loch Etchachan on Ben Muich Dhui, both having a tiny lochlet. Below, the channel of the burn is quite rocky, but smooth, often glistening in the summer sun. At the East end of the Lochan there is a little beach of silvery sand. It abounds, with trout larger even than those in Loch Muick, from which it was stocked in 1856 with two dozen. The remains of an old shooting hut of the Gordons of Abergeldie may still be traced below the Lochan.

The pony path from the Glasallt Shiel keeps by the left bank of the Muick - here - known by the name of Allt an Dubh Loch. From the Glasallt Shiel to the Dubh Loch the distance is about two miles, and the scenery is almost as magnificent as any in the Highlands. The mountains, composed of granite, on both sides of the burn which guides the way, are alike high and steep, and have a very graceful outline, while a few trees beautify the banks of the stream. About half-way between the Glasallt Shiel and the Dubh Loch, a tributary (the Allt an Lochan Buidhe) of the Allt an Dubh Loch is crossed, having a particularly fine waterfall known as the "Stullan". The bottom of this waterfall is close to the edge of the path, while near the junction of the burn with Allt an Dubh Loch

are the ruins of the farthest up smuggling bothy in Glen
Muick. A small cairn will attract attention as soon as
the tourist has crossed the Allt an Lochan Buidhe at
the bottom of the "Stullan". It is understood to
mark the spot where the Marquis of Lorne proposed
to the Princess Louise on the 3rd October, 1870. It
so happened that the Queen was at Pannanich Wells
that day!

The Dubh Loch is described by the Queen, on
her first visit to it in September, 1849, as "very wild;
the hills, which are very rocky and precipitous, rising
perpendicularly from it". In its grandeur and remote-
ness it will satisfy even the most exacting mountaineer. It is nearly three-quarters of a mile in length,
with an area of 60 acres, and is 2091 feet above sea
level. Broad Cairn (3268 feet) and Cairn Bannoch
(3314 feet), the latter with a distinctive peaked top,
overlook the Loch on the South and South-West.
These two mountains have stupendous granite precipices (Creag an Dubh Loch) which overhang the
water, and are the grandest on Lochnagar. Their
perpendicular height where highest is 800 feet, giving
the head of the Dubh Loch a resemblance, in a
measure, to the upper end of Loch Avon in the
vicinity of the Shelter Stone. The rocks on the
North-East side of the Loch do not approach the edge
of the water so closely as the crags on the South-West,
by which also they are surpassed in steepness. Both
have the same name, Creag an Dubh Loch; but
those on the North-East side are distinguished by
having Creag na h-Iolaire (the eagle's craig) as the
name of their highest point. Eagles had formerly
their eyries there, but it is long since they ceased to

frequent these rocks. A slender cataractrill which
falls over this craig has an almost perpendicular
descent of about 200 feet. The name of this burn is
the Allt a' Choire Bhoidheach (the burn of the beautiful corrie); it rises on the South side of the rocks
above Lochan an Eoin.

The Dubh Loch swarms with trout, of which 35
were brought from Loch Muick in 1852. From having

DUBH LOCH.

been left comparatively alone the size of the fish
considerably exceeds the size of those in Loch Muick;
and this is all the more remarkable as ice has been
found on the Dubh Loch as late in the summer as the
10th June. Stags when wounded frequently take
shelter in water. On one occasion when a hunting
party was out from Balmoral Castle, a wounded stag

swam to the centre of the Dubh Loch. None of the
company could swim except the Duke of Edinburgh,
so the Prince went in and gave the stag the *coup de
grace*. The antlers now adorn the outside of the
front door of Alltnaguibhsaich Lodge. While the
burn *from* the Dubh Loch has a picturesque and
romantic course over rocks and stones, the burn
entering  it has likewise a most interesting run. Just
above the Loch it slides, rather than flows, over
a great stretch of rock which gives it a peculiar
appearance. Farther up it rushes through a little
rocky gorge with here and there a small cascade. In
its upper parts it is, however, not particularly interesting. Its parent head-stream is the Allt na Da Chraobh
Bheath.

The best point from which to view the picturesque
features on the left bank of Loch Muick is from a
height of about 2100 feet on the South side opposite
the Glasallt Shiel. From the path on the right bank
of the Loch a track branches off a few yards west of
the Black Burn and leads to Bachnagairn, and it is by
this latter path that the view referred to is obtained.
Here the broad level strath of the Muick, blocked up
by the Coyles, is seen to advantage, with the winding
river in the centre. The narrow gorge of the Alltan
Dearg is also partly seen. But the view of the Glasallt
Shiel, just at one's feet, with its romantic surroundings,
is what will charm most. Indeed, no such view can be
got from any other point. The Shiel appears to stand
on a little green patch surrounded by trees and the
Loch, and is built on a miniature delta formed by the
burn. At the back of the Shiel the Glas Allt
looks like a thread of silver from its precipitous

descent, the famous "Falls" themselves being also seen dropping perpendicularly. How charmingly do the "Stullan" Burn and the Allt an Dubh Loch send down their waters tumbling in headlong flight! Lochan Buidhe is just seen in its little hollow, and a peep is obtained of the Dubh Loch; behind is Lochnagar - below is Loch Muick. One could scarcely wish for a grander view of mingled Highland scenery.

Bachnagairn is outside the scope of the present work, but as it has been so nearly approached a little information concerning it may be welcomed. It is a disused shooting-box on the right bank of the South Esk, fully a mile East of Loch Esk, on the property of Sir Allan Mackenzie. There is no house above it, and the nearest below is a keeper's dwelling over two miles down the river, near the commencement of the Capel Mounth in Forfarshire. The South Esk at Bachnagairn hurries along an exceedingly narrow defile clothed with larch trees. It is crossed there by a pony-bridge, on both sides of which there is a grand waterfall, the only drawback being that a proper view of both falls cannot be obtained at once. Concerning the South Esk here, a very short description, written so far back as 1678 - when Highland scenery was not esteemed as it is now - will suffice:- "A stream which cannot so properly be said to flow as to precipitate itself from the highest cliff of a mountain for about one hundred fathoms".

I would fain advise the mountaineer who wishes to see the beauties of Lochnagar from a new direction to take the point of view just indicated, returning to Spital by Bachnagairn (crossing the South Esk by a foot-bridge about a mile below the Falls) and the Capel

Mounth - the round can be made easily within six
hours. If he has ascended Lochnagar once or twice
the views obtained in this little circular tour will charm
him - or her, for a more pleasant mountain excursion
for ladies could not well be devised - and no regret
will be felt that a long distance has been come without
"doing" a mountain top. For I hold that the true
mountaineer is not the man who boasts of the number
of peaks he has placed to his credit; the ideal hillman
is one who thoroughly enjoys a day "on" the
mountains - not hurrying and toiling up a Ben with the
single purpose of rushing down again.

---

### THE  SPECTRE STAG OF LOCHNAGAR.

BY W. A. MacKenzie.

Up in the moonlight pale and dim
The Dubh Loch's cliffs rose stark and grim;
The loch gloomed darkling far beneath,
And weirdly strange lay height and heath ;
Deep silence held the mighty hill,
And all the wrestling winds were still;
The sky was bare save one lone star
That crowned the crest of Lochnagar.
Upon the black steep's topmost ken
There stood a Stag, a Stag of ten,
A lordly monarch of the wild
That hunters never had beguiled.
Such was the keenness of his sight
And scent, so swift his lightning flight,
So full of wile his quick resource,
No man might stay his whirlwind course.
From this his name was noised afar-
The Spectre Stag of Lochnagar-

Filled many a huntsman's heart with fire
That flamed to the supreme desire
To bring the noble beast to bay,
And take his ten-tined head that day.

Lord Ian was a huntsman keen
As ever donned the Lincoln green,
As ever led the chase at morn,
Or cheer'ly blew the ringing horn.
And countless trophies of his skill
In venery by plain and hill
Hung on the shield- and spear-sprent walls
Of his war-won ancestral halls.
Now when of this proud Stag he heard
His huntsman's soul was strangely stirred,
So at our holy Lady's shrine
He knelt, and craved her Grace divine
To lend the blessing of her eyes,
And consummate his vowed emprize-
To slay the Spectre Stag he swore,
Or hunting horn wind nevermore.

In yonder forest far away
He roused the Stag at dawn of day,
And following fast by tarn and rill,
O'er grassy slope and heathered hill,
All through the long autumnal heat,
He tracked him with unwearied feet,
Buoyed by elusive hope, till now
The monarch halts upon the brow
Of this rough crag, that stern doth loom
Over the Dubh Loch's rock-girt gloom,
Adown the proud beast's heaving side
Trickles a tiny crimson tide,
That shows where deep the arrow-head
Has sought and found its living bed.
With joy he sniffs the cool night air,
And dreams of his far forest lair,
And recks not that with bated breath
To deal the sudden stroke of death,

With eager longing in his eye,
While heart and hopes are pulsing high,
The hunter steals.    Aloft the knife
Shimmers to drink the Stag's red life.
But with a swerve like lightning's flash
The Stag makes one impetuous dash,
And from the sheer and fated steep
He takes the last, long, flying leap ;
A moment sways in dizzy air ;
Then, with a cry of shrill despair
Sinks swiftly to his lonely grave
Beneath the Dubh Loch's wind-swept wave.
The huntsman foiled, with frenzied eye,
Glares wildly to the silent sky,
And by some fascination held
Is to the shrinking brink compelled ;
Nor slacks the chase, nor draws he breath,
But onward still, till Huntsman Death
O'ertakes him too.

          The vow he swore
He kept; his horn sounds nevermore.

And to this hour, old shepherds say,
When moon and star succeed to day,
Is seen upon the Dubh Loch's scaur
The Spectre Stag of Lochnagar.

ALLTNAGUIBHSAICH LODGE.

# CHAPTER II. - *(Concluded)*

## BALLATER TO LOCHNAGAR.

*4. Alltnaguibhsaich Lodge to Cac Carn Beag.*

Hail, Lochnagar; thy precipices hail;
  Thy deep ravines; thy glittering wreaths of snow!
Thy forehead shrouded in a misty veil,
  Or darkly shadowed in the lake below.

ALLTNAGUIBHSAICH Lodge may be described as the key to Lochnagar from the East (the Ballater) side. The route passes the back of the Lodge by a path which branches off the approach just within the entrance gate. The stable and coach-house are within this gate, and it is at the West-end of these buildings that the path commences. Passing in rear of the Lodge, it comes out between the Keeper's house (a continuation of the Lodge) and a small building known as the Ghillies' Hall. A few yards ahead there is a little wooden gate in the deer fence; that gate passed through the mountain path begins. A finger-post at the entrance gate, and another at the deer fence, would prevent any chance of a stranger blundering, and the public would be saved from thoughtlessly or inadvertently passing the front of the Lodge, when occupied by visitors. Of course, for persons who will flatten their noses against window panes, the better to examine a private house, finger-posts would be superfluous. The path from the Lodge to the summit of Lochnagar was made by the Queen's directions in 1849, partly for Her Majesty's own use, and partly also to keep the public from unduly wandering in the Royal deer forests of Balmoral and the White Mounth. So early as 1850, Her Majesty had earned the reputation of having "the good taste to delight in mountaineering".

The path at first trends to the right, crossing the Allt na Guibhsaich a little above the Lodge. Two miles or so West of the Lodge a watershed is reached, where, on the right, the Gelder Bum has its principal source, and, on the left, is one of the head streams of the Allt na Guibhsaich. Here a path is crossed leading, on the right, to Balmoral Castle by Glen Gelder, and, on the left, to the Glasallt Shiel by the Moss of Monelpie and the Falls of the Glasallt. After crossing the watershed the climber will find that the track becomes considerably rougher, and the ascent may now be said to begin in earnest. Before him - at some little distance - is "the Ladder", which leads to the top of the ridge of Cuidhe Crom, and from it the path, after slightly dipping by the edge of the corrie of "Lochnagar", leads onward and upward to Cac Carn Mor. A quarter of a mile Northwards from this peak, with first a very slight dip and then a slight rise, Cac Carn Beag is reached.

Every mountaineer, on arranging to visit Lochnagar for the first time, is pretty sure to ask the question - How long does it require to reach the top of the mountain from Alltnaguibhsaich Lodge, and to return to the same point? It is, of course, quite impossible to reply in an off-hand manner; the question must be answered with a certain knowledge of the staying powers of the particular individual. Speaking in general terms, a fair mountaineer should reach the summit in two hours - it has to the writer's knowledge been done in half an hour less - and the descent should be made in about an hour and twenty minutes. But for ordinary pedestrians the writer quite agrees with Mr. Grierson, the *doyen* of mountaineers in the middle of the present century - than whom there could be no better authority - who says:- "The ascent and descent, including half an hour at the summit, cannot be comfortably accomplished under five or six hours - starting from or near the Hut". Of the four and a half miles which the pedestrian has to climb, mostly in a due West direction, the first and easiest half of the way lies between the Hut and the base of the Meikle Pap, the mean gradient for the whole distance being only about 1 in 7.

Having thus briefly indicated the final section of the route from Ballater to Lochnagar, it may be advantageous to describe a little more fully what may be properly enough termed the Queen's path from Alltnaguibhsaich Lodge to the summit of the mountain. The bridge crossing the Allt na Guibhsaich, a short distance above the Lodge, is known as Littlejohn's Bridge, from the name of the builder. The remains of several shielings may be seen near by, telling of the time when the natives of Glen Muick summered their cattle on the pastures by the higher burns along the glen. Marks of the foundations of a smuggling bothy may be seen immediately above the bridge. This is believed to have been the highest situated "black" bothy on the Allt na Guibhsaich. Beyond Littlejohn's Bridge the path lies on the Southern shoulder of Conachcraig. This name most probably

signifies Kenneth's Craig, but it may also mean the
dogs' or the stormy craig. Granite millstones would
appear to have been at one time quarried on it, as
several half-finished stones are still lying on the slope.
A few yards above the bridge, at a height of about
1680 feet, there is a big stone on the right bank of the
burn, near which, on looking backwards towards the
East, Mount Keen just begins to appear behind the hills
on the right bank of the Muick. A few yards farther
on, the cone will be plainly recognisable. The view
now deserves particular attention, as an altitude has
been reached that affords a fair prospect. Looking
back, the tree-girt Lodge is visible; the Allt Darrarie
in its deep, narrow glen is seen joining the Muick at
Spital; and the great hollow containing Loch Muick
forces itself upon the eye. Looking forward and upwards there is the peaked Little Pap and the more
massive but less picturesque Cuidhe Crom. The
region of trees, save for a straggler here and there by
the burnside, has been left behind. The mountaineer
will scarcely have ascended another hundred feet above
sea level when Meikle Pap, on the right of Cuidhe
Crom, will come into view, as well as *the* crags of
Lochnagar itself. On the extreme right of Cuidhe
Crom the zig-zag path, "the Ladder", may be picked
out.

About a mile-and-a-quarter above the Lodge a
suitable place may be observed for a short halt. This is
at "Cameron's Well", on the right of the path, the deep
narrow hollow in which flows the Allt na Guibhsaich
being on the left. From this point the peculiarly cut
rocky top of the Meikle Pap will show itself; beyond
it "the    steep frowning glories of dark Lochnagar"

begin to inspire the tourist on his maiden ascent of Byron's mountain. Little of the crags will be seen from this point, but quite sufficient to arouse one's curiosity and expectation. The gorge of the burn is known as Clashrathan, a word which signifies the hollow of the roads, there being numerous deer tracks or roads along the stream. Behind, the brown and green hills at the head of Loch Muick will attract attention, as well as a little bit of the glen at Spital, and Mount Keen, now fully in view in the East in all his conical dignity.

A few hundred yards farther onward, at a height of about 2180 feet, one of the principal summits of the Cairngorm mountains comes into view - Ben Avon with his rocky pinnacles. These pinnacles are visible from great distances - particularly from the Blue Hill in Banchory-Devenick, a distance of about 48 miles - and they enable one readily to pick out the giant mountain which derives its name from the river Avon.

"Clashrathan's Cairn" at the watershed of the Gelder marks the point for a divergence in the route to the summit, at the crossing of the path which leads from Balmoral Castle to the Glasallt Shiel. Looking Northward from this cairn, Ben Avon comes better into view, as well as one of his spurs, Meall na Gaineimh, which almost overhangs Inchrory Lodge. Culardoch, a mountain on the South side of the Gairn, is also now very prominent. To the right is Conach-craig, sloping down on the East side of the Gelder to Balmoral Castle.

Having reached the head of Gelder Burn, the Glen Gelder route to the summit of Lochnagar may be briefly referred to. It is the most direct route from Easter Balmoral and the neighbourhood of Balmoral

Castle, and joins the Alltnaguibhsaich Lodge path at
the watershead of the Gelder and the head stream of
the Allt na Guibhsaich just mentioned. There is no
difficulty in following it; but it must be kept in mind
that it is not always open to the public, and care
should therefore be taken to make the necessary
inquiries before proceeding by that route. It mostly
suits only the inhabitants in the district of Crathie.
Her Majesty has a small "Shiel" in this glen some
three miles from the watershed, known as the Glen
Gelder Shiel, or Ruidh na Bhan Righ (the Queen's
Shiel), concerning a visit to which, with the Empress
Eugenie in 1879, Her Majesty thus writes:- "The
Empress was pleased with the little Shiel, which contains only two small rooms and a little kitchen. It
stands in a very wild, solitary spot, looking up to
Lochnagar, which towers up immediately above the
house. . . . We walked along the footpath above the
Gelder for a mile and a half, the dogs, which had
come up, following us, and the Empress talked a great
deal, and most pleasantly, about former times. When
we came back to the little Shiel, after walking for an
hour, we had tea. Brown had caught some excellent
trout and cooked them with oatmeal, which the dear
Empress liked extremely, and said would be her dinner.
It was a glorious evening - the hills pink, and the sky
so clear".

Another "minor" route converges at the head of
Glen Gelder - that, namely, by Strath Girnock from
the North-East. This route may best be entered near
the mouth of the Strath, about two miles West of
Knock Castle. The head of the Strath reached, Glen
Gelder will be entered between Conachcraig and

Little Conachcraig (1841 feet). It is, however, of little public convenience, and the Strath is now very sparsely inhabited. Formerly it was particularly noted for smuggling, no fewer than a dozen or so of "black bothies" being at one time in operation in the upper part of the little glen. There is yet living a native of the district who can recollect of a line of thirty horses starting from Strath Girnock, loaded with smuggled whisky, *en route* for the South by Capel Mounth. A road, already referred to, crosses the Girnock, about a mile-and-a-half below its source, leading Northwards to the Dee at Easter Balmoral, and Southwards to the Muick at Inschnabobart.

Returning again to the main route to Cac Carn Beag at the head of Glen Gelder, the mountaineer will pass on his right the ruins of what was formerly a little "box" of the Queen's. It had a stable attached for ponies, but was demolished in 1867. Tourists occasionally abused it, and the Glen Gelder Shiel was consequently built, in a less exposed position. The corrie to the North of the ruins, at the foot of the Meikle Pap, is called Coire na Ciche (the corrie of the pap), and shows pretty conclusively that Meikle Pap is but a translation from the Gaelic "Ciche Mhor". The Prince Consort shot his last stag on Meikle Pap, and a small cairn (on the North-East side from the mountain path) was raised to mark the spot. A small tarn, known as Lochan Dubh, in Coire na Ciche, is the source of one of the head streams of the Gelder Burn, the principal one issuing from the Loch of Lochnagar on the West side of Meikle Pap.

About half way between Alltnaguibhsaich Lodge and Cac Carn Beag another "Well" will be passed on the left. It is known as the Fox Cairn Well, and it may be interesting to mention that the natural mass of big granite stones, so called, derived its name from a fox that was killed there in 1840. This particular wily reynard was an old grey animal which was almost toothless, but had played such havoc among a certain sheep-farmer's flocks, that his loss was competently estimated at no less a sum than £100. This statement may appear somewhat extreme, but it has to be recollected that the whole district suffered exceedingly at one time from the depredations of foxes and other vermin. It is on record that previous to 1776 the destruction of sheep by vermin was so great in the parishes of Braemar, Crathie, Glenmuick, Tullich and Glengairn, that the loss was estimated as nearly equal to half the rent paid to the proprietors. To prevent this loss the landowners in 1776 entered into an agreement, whereby premiums were offered for the destruction of the vermin, and these were paid for ten years. During that period, 634 foxes, 44 wild cats, 57 pole-cats, 70 eagles, 2520 hawks and kites, and 1347 ravens and hooded crows were killed at a cost of about forty guineas a year. When the proprietors, grudging the expense, dropped the agreement, the vermin once more gained ground, and sheep suffered correspondingly. Fox-hunting was an occupation then, and one of the famous hunters of the district, Samuel Copland, was known to have killed over 700 foxes in a period of about eleven years. These facts will indicate how the recesses of Lochnagar were inhabited over a hundred years ago.

The water from the Fox Cairn Well finds its way below the stones to the Gelder, but certainly to the casual observer it has rather the appearance of making its way to the Allt na Guibhsaich. Several cairns, which may still be observed in the neighbourhood, pointed the route to the summit before the Queen's path was formed. A halt had better be made by the Well, for this is the last opportunity of drinking spring water till the summit is reached, and it has to be borne in mind that "the Ladder" - the only really steep part of the ascent - is just ahead. This expression, "the Ladder", is by no means peculiar to Lochnagar; mention need only be made of "the Ladder" on Donside, and "the Ladder" on the South side of Mount Keen.

When the foot of "the Ladder" has been reached, the list of mountains visible will include the well-known Morven, and the still more famous Bennachie, although the latter is of considerably lower elevation. Before tackling "the Ladder", the tourist will have observed that the track has materially deteriorated from what it was below Clashrathan's Cairn. It is now distinguished by narrow ruts, wide apart, not un-like wheel marks, the better to enable one to keep the track should mist overtake the unwary mountaineer. Having surmounted "the Ladder" and landed on the ridge of Cuidhe Crom (the crooked or bent [snow] wreath), the traveller may well take another halt, and make a few yards' diversion from the path, the better to see the great corrie of Lochnagar, with the loch lying so serenely at a height of nearly 2600 feet, almost en-circled by mighty precipices. *These* are "the steep frowning glories of dark Lochnagar"; and when the mountaineer is brought fairly face to face with them, he is not likely to be disappointed with the realisation of the expectations raised by the peeps obtained of the broken line of their crest as he ascended. Above, and a little beyond the top of the crags on the West side of the loch, he will have no difificulty in recognising the goal of his journey, the Cac Carn Beag. But before he can arrive at that well-defined peak, the corrie in which the loch is set has to be rounded, and in rounding it Cac Carn Mor will first be reached. At the latter terminates, in an upward direction, the mountain path, and five minutes walk will now take the climber to Cac Carn Beag, the summit of Loch-nagar; and the peak so prominent from innumerable points will at last be surmounted.

# CHAPTER III.

## BALLATER TO BRAEMAR.

*I. Ballater to Crathie.*

Bonnie lassie, will ye go
To the Birks o' Abergeldie?

THE route between Ballater and Braemar is perhaps
the finest in Aberdeenshire - certainly in the summer
and autumn months it is more frequented than any
other similar length of road (about 16½ miles) in the
county. What more concerns the Lochnagar tourist,
who proposes to make Braemar the base for the ascent,
is the fact that from the road the mountain is very
well seen for several miles. From Ballater it is particularly prominent, the picturesque contour and the
magnificent corries of the White Mounth constantly
compelling the admiration of the traveller as he proceeds along the North side of the Dee.

Until the purchase of the estate of Balmoral by
Prince Albert, there was a public road on both banks of
the river between Ballater and Braemar. As, however,
the South road ran through the estate and past the
Castle, an arrangement was made with the Road
Trustees, acting on behalf of the public, for having
that road shut up from the point where it reached the
entrance to the Balmoral grounds, about eight miles
from Ballater, to the West-end of the Ballochbuie
Forest (now part of the Balmoral estate) at the Bridge
of Dee. That arrangement included the building of a

substantial bridge over the Dee, as well as the improve-
ment and widening of the North road, these works
being carried out at the Prince's expense. These con-
siderations might not have prevented all opposition to
the closing of some seven miles of a beautiful old
highway, but it was plain that if an agreement to that
effect was not concluded, the Queen could not con-
tinue to live on Deeside if the privacy of her house
and grounds were not to be assured. The arrangement was finally completed by a private Act of Parliament.

The South road has already been noticed as far as
Knock Castle. Abergeldie Castle is also on the South
side of the Dee, and it, and other interesting points,
will be taken in order as we proceed by the North
road - which is the shorter and better of the two.

A short distance from the railway station (on the
left) stand the Barracks, erected to accommodate the
Guard of Honour kept on Deeside while Her Majesty
is resident at Balmoral. Seldom indeed are the soldiers
near the Castle, and so far as there is any real "guarding"
of the Queen during her stay on Deeside, the duty is
entrusted to a very few men of the "A" Division of the
Metropolitan Police Force, under an Inspector, who
travels with the Royal train, and who may be observed
taking post near Her Majesty's saloon when the train
makes a brief halt at Ferryhill (Aberdeen) or other
places on the journey. The sending of soldiers to
Deeside was begun about twenty years ago. At first
they were lodged with the villagers in Ballater, and in
the summer and autumn they certainly did not get the
best of the houses. Ever mindful of her soldiers, the
Queen sent one of her physicians to see how they

lived in Ballater, and the report he gave of their enforced sleeping places is stated to have led to the
building of the Barracks. The style of the structure is
not considered to be in keeping with the locality, and
a story was told to the effect that the plans used for
Ballater were really intended for a cantonment in India,
while India had sent to it the plans drawn for Deeside!

Craigendarroch (the hill of the oaks) rises to a
height of about 1360 feet to the right of the road, and
the ascent along its base is rather stiff for a turnpike.
It is understood that, but for trouble being feared from land-
slips, the road would have been constructed nearer
the river, and the gradient would then have been very
easy. After the highest point is reached there is a fall to
the Bridge of Gairn. On the left side may be observed a
short railway track. Power was asked from Parliament
about 1864 to make a line to Braemar, but it was
opposed by the Earl of Fife and the Balmoral Trustees,
and legislative sanction was only granted to Bridge of
Gairn, about a mile-and-a-half West from Ballater.
Rails were laid down to that point, with the intention
that the track beyond Ballater should be used for
timber and other goods traffic. The project proved
unsuitable, and the rails were lifted two or three years
ago. There is a deep narrow gorge on the North side
of Craigendarroch known as the "Pass of Ballater",
along which the North turnpike ran before the village
of Ballater was built. The old road (*via* the Pass)
and the new (via Ballater) join about a quarter-of-a-
mile East of the Bridge of Gairn.

Near where the railway track ends is the churchyard of Glengairn, with the ruins of the old Church.
The ancient Church of Glengairn was dedicated to St.

Mungo, and it is understood to have been a separate
charge till about 1740. Curiously enough, however,
neither the site of the old manse nor the glebe can
now be pointed out. The Church and Manse of the
*quoad sacra* parish of Glengairn are farther up the
river Gairn, which is generally regarded as the largest
tributary of the Dee. The bridge that carries the
turnpike over the Gairn is close to the churchyard.
The ruins of its predecessor are noticeable a few yards
up the stream.

About three-and-a-half-miles from Ballater is the snug
little inn of Coillecriech. Almost opposite it (on the
South side of the river) is the mouth of Strath Girnock
(one of the "minor" routes to the summit of Lochnagar), with its two guardian, pine-clothed hills. The inn
is regarded as a very convenient halting point for men
and horses. Looking backward from this point there
is a capital view of Craigendarroch, with the deep cut
of the Pass. South of the Dee rise the green-topped
Coyles of Muick. Forward from Coillecriech there
seems to be an amphitheatre surrounded by hills, all
more or less rocky and picturesquely clad with heather,
pine, and birch.

A little below the forty-seventh milestone, on the
right hand side of the road, on the West side of Easter
Micras Burn, may still be seen indications of the site
of the old Roman Catholic Chapel of Micras. The
site can be readily found by a standing stone that is
placed at its West end - a stone which is believed to
have formed part of a Druidical circle long before the
introduction of Christianity into Upper Deeside by
St. Nathalan. The Chapel stood at the base of
Geallaig (the white mountain), which, rising to a height

of 2170 feet above sea level, is the most prominent hill close to the North side of the turnpike between Ballater and Crathie. The old Chapel supplied religious services for the residents in the two hamlets of Easter and Wester Micras, on the North side of the turnpike. For some occult reason Micras was not held in great esteem, and was generally referred to as "the village opposite Abergeldie". A quarter of a century or so ago, it was a genuine specimen of a Highland clachan of the poorest type.

Six miles from Ballater (within a hundred and fifty yards of the 48th milestone), the tourist will find himself opposite the Castle of Abergeldie on the South side of the Dee. At one time, however, the Castle had been on the North side of the river; marks of the old course are still traceable. The Castle is not imposing, but is picturesquely situated on the right bank of the Geldie Burn. It was formerly the property of the Mowat family, but now belongs to Mr. Hugh Mackay Gordon. "The Birks o' Abergeldie" are celebrated in an old song which Burns transformed into the beautiful lyric, "The Birks o' Aberfeldy". The Castle and lands are held in lease by the Queen, and it is understood that all overtures for their purchase have been declined. Abergeldie estate is contiguous to that of Balmoral, and the two would make a very compact property, especially when it is considered that Birkhall, also belonging to the Queen, lies next to Abergeldie on the East, and near to the Balmoral Forest at its South-Eastern boundary. Her Majesty's mother, the Duchess of Kent, occupied Abergeldie Castle for many years as an autumn residence, and in more recent times it has been tenanted

by the Prince and Princess of Wales. Now it is retained by the Queen for distinguished visitors, and the
Empress Eugenie has on more than one occasion
lived in it during the autumn months. The front of
the Castle faces the South road, and at the edge of the
road opposite the Castle there is an uninscribed
standing stone, some six feet in height. Communica-
tion between the Castle and the North side of the
Dee was formerly maintained by means of a "cradle",
running on a rope suspended from posts at each side
of the river. About 150 years ago an exciseman
named Bruce, anxious to get at some smugglers he
believed to be at Clachanturn, lost his life by the
accidental breaking of the rope when the Dee was in
flood. This was followed by a more memorable and
- naturally - more lamented occurrence, the death of
a recently married couple, Peter Frankie, the gamekeeper at the "Hut", and Barbara Brown, while
crossing by the "cradle". The cause of this "accident"
remained a mystery, but it was attributed by some to
the malignancy of a disappointed suitor of "Babby's".
In 1885 a handsome suspension foot-bridge was erected
over the Dee to give access to the Castle. A remark
made by the Rev. Dr. George Skene Keith, in his
*Agricultural Survey of Aberdeenshire*, should interest
visitors to Upper Deeside, if not the Lochnagar
mountaineer. When the worthy divine was at Abergeldie, in 1810, it was in the occupation of Captain
and Mrs. Gordon, and the Doctor wrote that their
"excellent birch wine appeared to me superior to the finest
champagne". Birch trees are probably as numerous as ever in the locality, but the making of wine
from them is a lost art.

ABERGELDIE CASTLE AND SUSPENSION BRIDGE.

Craig nam Ban (the women's craig - 1730 feet) slopes on the South-East to Abergeldie Castle. On the summit may still be seen the mark of the hollow where a stake was fixed to which witches were bound on being burned. There is also a ring in a vault in the Castle where they, and other "criminals", were chained up during their imprisonment.

Within a mile of Abergeldie Castle, to the South, on the left bank of the Geldie Burn, may be seen the site of St. Columba's Chapel, with a small burial-ground, fringed with trees, around it. The walls of the Church are completely gone, and no tombstones are to be seen; indeed, the casual observer would pass by without distinguishing the site. The field in which the Church stood is, however, still known as Chapel Park. The last burial is said to have taken place about 150 years ago, and was that of a soldier, known, from the colour of his facings, as the "Blue Drummer". About the same time the Abergeldie tenants removed, for building purposes, part of the walls of the Church and the surrounding dyke. This act of vandalism was accomplished before means could be taken at the Castle to save the ruins of the holy edifice, but it is believed that the present dyke was erected, and the trees planted, by order of the wife of the then laird.

Like the other lands on Upper Deeside, Abergeldie originally formed part of the Earldom of Mar. About the year 1507 the Crown, as coming in place of the old Earls of Mar, laid claim to Abergeldie, but the Privy Council found that these lands were "distinct landes fra the Erledome of Marr". In the beginning of the sixteenth century Sir Alexander Gordon of Midmar, a son of the Earl of Huntly, received a charter of the lands of Abergeldie and Estoun, and the property is still in the possession of the same branch of the Gordon family.

The Church of Crathie is passed nearly eight miles

CRATHIE CHURCH.

from Ballater. It stands on the right hand side of the North road, and is a plain - almost barn-like - building erected in 1805-6, but the Queen has enriched it with stained-glass windows in memory of the Rev. Dr. Norman Macleod. Till within the last three years Her Majesty worshipped regularly in this Church every Sunday during her stay at Balmoral, but latterly the behaviour of tourists from a distance compelled the Queen to cease attending regularly. In consequence Her Majesty has built a "worship room" in Balmoral Castle, where some distinguished minister of the Church of Scotland is invited to conduct the services. In the month of October, however, the Queen attends Crathie Church on the Sacrament Sabbath.

# CHAPTER III. - *(Continued.)*

## BALLATER TO BRAEMAR.

*2. Crathie to Inver.*

On to the gentle Lady's halls
Who wears old Scotland's crown.

THE site of the old Church of Crathie is on the left side of the road, almost opposite the new building.

In olden times the Church of Crathie belonged to the Abbey of Cambuskenneth. The ruins of the ancient structure, now clad with ivy, stand in the parish burial-ground nearly midway between the North Road and the Dee, and the manse is close beside them. They are on the right hand side of a road which leads from the North road to a suspension bridge for foot passengers over the river. This bridge superseded a ferry at Clachanturn, fully half-a-mile farther down the river, and is about twelve feet in width. It is inscribed :-

J. JUSTICE JUNR & CO
DUNDEE
1834

Crathie churchyard, thanks to the Queen, is very neatly kept, and, like the whole district, it bears evidence of Her Majesty's affectionate character and of her kindly remembrance of faithful service. A number of the gravestones are inscribed as having been raised by the Queen in memory of servants in the Royal household. Among these monuments the one that will attract most attention is the stone which marks the grave of John Brown. The family of which he was a member had belonged to the Parish for generations as is attested by stones erected in 1827 and 1859, as well as by a stone which Brown himself caused to be raised in memory of his parents and other relations. The four "lairs" assigned to the Browns are now enclosed within a neat iron railing. The stone put up by the Queen is entirely in keeping with the one erected by Brown. Musicians will note with interest a stone inscribed to the memory of "William Blair, house carpenter and violinist, who died, at Belnacroft, Abergeldie, Nov. 12, 1884, aged 90 years". Willie Blair, the Queen's fiddler (as he was long termed in familiar and kindly phrase), played at the festive gatherings held in the old and new ballrooms at Balmoral Castle for more than thirty years; and all over "the country side" his powers were known, and his fame was firmly established, a third of a century before Her Majesty had made a home for herself under the shadow of Lochnagar.

The Free Church of Crathie is half-a-mile to the South of Crathie churchyard, on the opposite side of the river. Its pretty spire is seen rising through the trees when looked for from the road on the North side of the Dee.

The Lochnagar Distillery stands a few yards West of the Free Church of Crathie, within a mile of Balmoral Castle. One of the earliest of the "sma' still" whisky makers, of whom distinct record remains in the Lochnagar district, was "Strowan Robertson". His death in 1812 at the age of 52 is inscribed on a table-stone in the churchyard of Glenmuick, and it is there stated that he was "some time miller at Mill of Balmoral". Charles was his Christian name, and the patronymic "Strowan" was assigned him from the family property of the Robertsons (Dundonnachie) in Atholl. In 1825 James Robertson of Crathie - an old smuggler - erected the first regular distillery on Upper Deeside. It stood near the site of the suspension bridge, and was an insignificant building covered with wood. About 1838 the distillery was removed to its present site. James Robertson was succeeded by the laird of Abergeldie himself, but he soon let it to one William Farquharson. The latter transferred his interest to the firm of Begg & Buyers, and thereafter started another distillery at Balnacroft, Abergeldie, which was not long in use. The firm that succeeded Farquharson was by and by solely represented by the senior partner, on whose death the present occupant came into possession. The Distillery being on the Abergeldie estate the distiller is a sub-tenant to the Queen.

Balmoral Castle stands on the South side of the Dee, on a narrow strip of level ground, about equidistant from Ballater and Braemar. The site has been found fault with, on account of its lowness and proximity to the river; otherwise one would be inclined to say that the situation is perfection. Its surroundings are magnificent. The Castle is embosomed among birches, while pines rise above it on the slope of Lochnagar (which it faces), and at its base on the North side is the river Dee - its clear stream there rushing briskly along. The building, the site, and the surroundings are alike grand; and no one who knows them will wonder why Her Majesty spends such a considerable portion of the year on Deeside. The Castle is in the Scottish Baronial style of architecture, but with several deviations and innovations, which tend to assure the greater comfort and accommodation of the residents. Thus the building partly displays the characteristics of an ancient stronghold and partly those of a modern residence. Prince Albert (it is understood) designed the main features of the Castle, and the plans were supplied by Mr. William Smith, who has held the appointment of City Architect of Aberdeen for a long period. The Castle consists of two blocks connected by wings; a tower, which rises to the height of one hundred feet, is situated at the Eastern extremity. The building has an unusually bright appearance from being built of finely dressed granite of a light grey colour, obtained within a short distance. The granite is treated with a severe yet elegant simplicity and chasteness of design, with exquisiteness of workmanship. One writer says if you wish to see it in all its splendour you must come in a clear moonlight night, when it stands out in white relief from the dark mass of the surrounding trees and the deep shadow of the neighbouring hills, and when the particles of mica which the stones contain sparkle like silver as the cold stones are kissed by the chill moonbeams. Many additions have been made to the Castle within the past 30 years, and now the whole buildings afford accommodation for about 120 persons. The furnishings are plain, but in the finest taste.

The estate of Balmoral formerly belonged to the Farquharsons of Inverey, a branch of the Invercauld Farquharsons, from whom it was acquired by the Earl of Fife. The Earl's trustees leased the property to the

OLD CASTLE OF BALMORAL IN 1850.

Right Hon. Sir Robert Gordon, brother of the (Premier) Earl of Aberdeen, in the second quarter of the present century. Sir Robert Gordon added considerably to the small "house" which he found on the estate, and the "old castle" had latterly a somewhat imposing appearance. When Sir Robert died in 1847 Prince Albert acquired the reversion of his lease. For several years the Prince had been looking for an estate in the North of Scotland whereon a summer and autumn residence for the Queen could be provided, and Upper Deeside had been recommended by physicians and others as the most suitable locality. On 8th September, 1848, Her Majesty first arrived at Balmoral, after having landed at Aberdeen. Some years afterwards Prince Albert bought the estate, which stretches to the summit of Lochnagar. The price was £31,500. As the old castle proved quite inadequate for the royal requirements, the erection of a new structure was resolved upon, and on 28th September, 1853, the Queen laid the foundation-stone of the present building, which was completed in August, 1856. As is well known the estate is now the property of the Queen, and Her Majesty increased its extent several years ago on the West by purchasing Ballochbuie Forest from Invercauld. Including Birkhall on the East (bought for the Prince of Wales when he was comparatively young, and lately acquired from him by the Queen) the Royal lands on Deeside extend to between 40,000 and 50,000 acres. All this is private property, and not in any sense a possession of the Crown.

Reference has already been made to many memorials erected by the Queen, and numerous others could be mentioned. Perhaps two should be specially noted here. The first is a cairn of pyramidal form on Creag an Lurachain (1437 feet) - one

PRINCE ALBERT'S CAIRN.

of the tops of Creag a' Ghobhainn (the blacksmith's craig), better known as Craig Gowan, which rises immediately to the South of Balmoral Castle. This Cairn is a prominent object to the traveller passing along the North Deeside road. A number of the stones are marked with initials, representing all the members of the Royal Family.     The tablet is thus inscribed:-

TO THE BELOVED  MEMORY
OF
ALBERT, THE GREAT AND GOOD
PRINCE CONSORT,
RAISED  BY  HIS  BROKEN HEARTED  WIDOW,
VICTORIA R.
AUGUST 21, 1862,
"He being made perfect in a short time, fulfilled a long
    time:
For his soul pleased the Lord,
Therefore hastened He to take him
Away from among the wicked."
*Wisdom of Solomon, iv. 13, 14.*

STATUE OF THE QUEEN AT BALMORAL.

The other memorial is a bronze statue of the Prince Consort, by Theed, which stands on a high granite pedestal in an enclosed planting East from the entrance to the Castle, and may just be discerned among the trees. Facing it is a bronze statue of the Queen, erected three years ago by the tenantry and the servants on the Queen's Deeside estates and in the Royal Household. Near these statues is an obelisk raised to the memory of the Prince Consort soon after his death by the tenantry on the estates of Balmoral, Birkhall, and Abergeldie.

About a mile beyond Balmoral, to the North of the road, stood the original house of Monaltrie, the property of the Farquharsons. It was burned while in the occupancy of Government troops, after the battle of Culloden. Subsequently another house bearing the same name was erected under the shadow of Craigendarroch, immediately at the East end of the Pass of Ballater. The small "clachan" called the Street of Monaltrie was built for some of the old Highland soldiers on their return from the American wars. It is about a mile Westward from the site of the old house. Veins of fluor-spar in granite have been found in this neighbourhood.

Carn na Cuimhue (the cairn of remembrance) is the next object that will interest the tourist. It is a rough cairn of small stones surmounted by a flag-staff and vane. A low stone dyke, within which are planted a few trees, encloses the cairn, which is on the left-hand side of the road and close to the North bank of the river. "Carn na Cuimhue" was the "slogan" of the Farquharsons. The story regarding it is that when each clansman attended at the muster ground he brought a stone which he laid down near the cairn. The survivors, on their return from the expedition to which they had been summoned, each removed a stone from the subsidiary heap, and the stones left in it answered to the number of the slain and were added to *the* cairn. Opposite the cairn (on the South side-of the Dee) is the mouth of the Gelder Burn. The ascent of Lochnagar, the Dee forded, may at certain seasons be advantageously made from this point, despite a modern guide-book's direction that it "should not be attempted without a guide". Lochnagar is well seen here. Towards Inver, to the South-Westward of Carn na Cuimhue, the rocks are quartzose gniess, hornblende rock, bluish gray granular limestone and granite.

About a mile West of Carn na Cuimhue the Deeside road crosses the Feardar Burn at Mill of Inver, along which burn, in an upward direction, is the district of Aberarder. A quarter-of-a-mile farther along the main road is the Invercauld Arms, better known as Inver Inn. It is not a large building, but it is a favourite resort for tourists during the season. A former host, who rejoiced in the sobriquet of "Civil Bonnets", was a well-known character in his day. Opposite the Inn, on the South side of the Dee, is Canup Hill (1477 feet), which is surmounted by the Princess Royal's Cairn. A few yards West of the Inn a peep may be had of the rocky summits of Ben Avon.

# CHAPTER III. - *(Concluded.)*

## BALLATER TO BRAEMAR.

*3. Inver to Castleton.*

The standard's on the Braes of Mar,
Its ribands streaming rarely;
The gathering pipes on Lochnagar,
They're sounding lang and sarely.

WESTWARD of Inver Inn for about a couple of miles the pine and birch bordered road runs through a monotonously flat strip known as the Muir of Inver. On the South side of the river the Ballochbuie Forest affords shelter to deer and various kinds of game. Passing a wooden bridge, a little below the 55th milestone, which was thrown across the Dee for the purpose of carting cut timber from the Forest, and which now gives access from the North to the Danzig Shiel, a small lodge of the Queen's situated in the recesses of the Forest, the traveller will observe on his left, and only a short distance from the road, the old Bridge of Dee, which is 55½ miles from Aberdeen. Here, according to Dr. Macgillivray, the bed of the river is obliquely intersected by a broken ridge of slaty rock, causing a succession of little falls and rapids. The bridge was erected in 1752 by General Wade, in connection with his military road from Blairgowrie by Corgarff and Grantown to Inverness. It was built of stones obtained from Craig Clunie, on the South side of the Dee, in the vicinity. The bridge is now the property of the Queen, and connects the private road (formerly a part of the South Deeside turnpike) with the North Deeside road. The public are allowed the use of the bridge and the private road to visit the Falls of the Garbh Allt (rough burn), and an old retainer is stationed at the lodge at the North end of the bridge to see that this liberty is not abused.

The Falls of the Garbh Allt are within the Ballochbuie Forest, fully a mile South-East from the old Bridge of Dee. They are well worth seeing, being generally considered the most picturesque falls on Deeside, although the burn is inconsiderable in volume, and the falls which are three in number, are by no means remarkable for height. The bed of the burn is exceedingly rocky, and its banks are overhung by pines and birches; but the grandeur and solitude of the Falls are marred, according to some authorities on the picturesque, by a cast-iron bridge with a bow arch thrown across the stream just above the uppermost fall.

Above the Falls two burns (the Feindallacher and the Allt Lochan an Eoin) unite to form the Garbh Allt, and between these burns, up the Northern slope of Lochnagar, stretches the "Smuggler's Shank", an old route towards Glen Doll and Glen Clova in Forfarshire. This "Shank" received its name from having been in former times much used by smugglers to convey whisky on horseback from Deeside to the South. It is maintained by some that there is a right-of-way by this route through the Ballochbuie Forest to Lochnagar and the upper glens of the South Esk, but the question is not now likely to be raised. Mountaineers occasionally use this route when Her Majesty is not in the district.

Smuggling has had to be frequently mentioned in

connection with Lochnagar and its glens. An anonymous writer in the beginning of the present century
(the author of *A Summer Ramble in the North Highlands*) has some interesting remarks on the subject.
He states that in the glens and mountain nooks bor-
dering on the rivers Dee and Don, illicit distillation
"is the chief dependence of the peasantry; consequently
in no quarter of Scotland does it prevail to a greater
extent". He declares that the natives themselves
assert that though the penalty were death they must
still risk it, as they could not otherwise raise money to
supply the exactions of their landlords. At the period
referred to, as readers scarcely need be reminded, it
was not deemed in any sense a reproach to speak of a
man as a smuggler or a poacher. In fact, so common
and so rooted was the custom of illicitly distilling
whisky in Upper Deeside, that even the female farm
and domestic servants had considerable interest in the
practice. The reason for this is obvious - it gave the
servant a common interest with the master in keeping
the "gauger" from making unpleasant discoveries.

Parenthetically a few sentences may be set down
here to indicate why Highlanders were so remarkable
for their distrust of strangers, and why they were so
extremely reticent in giving precise information regarding localities and distances. When it became necessary that the laws for collecting duty upon all
whisky manufactured should be strictly enforced, a
system of espionage was introduced which made opera-
tions with "sma' stills" doubly hazardous, and consequently increased the precautions and the watchful-
ness necessary to evade detection. Of course the regular
"gauger" was well known in his own district, and his

every movement was observed and informed about.
But there were "rangers" in addition, and these
"rangers" rode wherever they listed, and thus became
enemies against whom foresight could not always avail.
The inhabitants of the glens compared them to the
bloodhound, hunting silently and secretly; pouncing
on their prey in the most sequestered spots and at the
most unlikely hours. The possible visits of these
officers created a prodigious antipathy to strangers
among the naturally hospitable peasantry; and every
person whose face was not quite familiar, or whose
coat appeared cut in a fashion at variance with the
taste of the country tailors, was viewed with suspicion,
and often received treatment of the kind that Bailie
Nicol Jarvie described as "the North side o' friendly".

Returning to the old Bridge of Dee, the traveller
may observe opposite it, on the North side of the
road, the entrance gate to Invercauld House. Strangely
enough the Farquharsons of Invercauld are the only
survivors, albeit by the female line, of the old families
of Braemar. Befitting such an ancient Highland
family, the mansion-house is a princely building, both
externally and internally, and is unrivalled for situation.
The style of the building is the Scottish Baronial, the
principal feature being a tower, surmounted by battle-
ments, which rises to the height of about 70 feet. In the
year 1875 the house was greatly enlarged - indeed
almost reconstructed - but the old historic dining-hall
is still almost the same as in the time of the Stewarts.
The view from the house is superb. The Dee, winding
through a narrow valley carpeted with green, can be
followed for miles. To the South rise tree-clad rocks
and crags, discernible   among   them being the mist

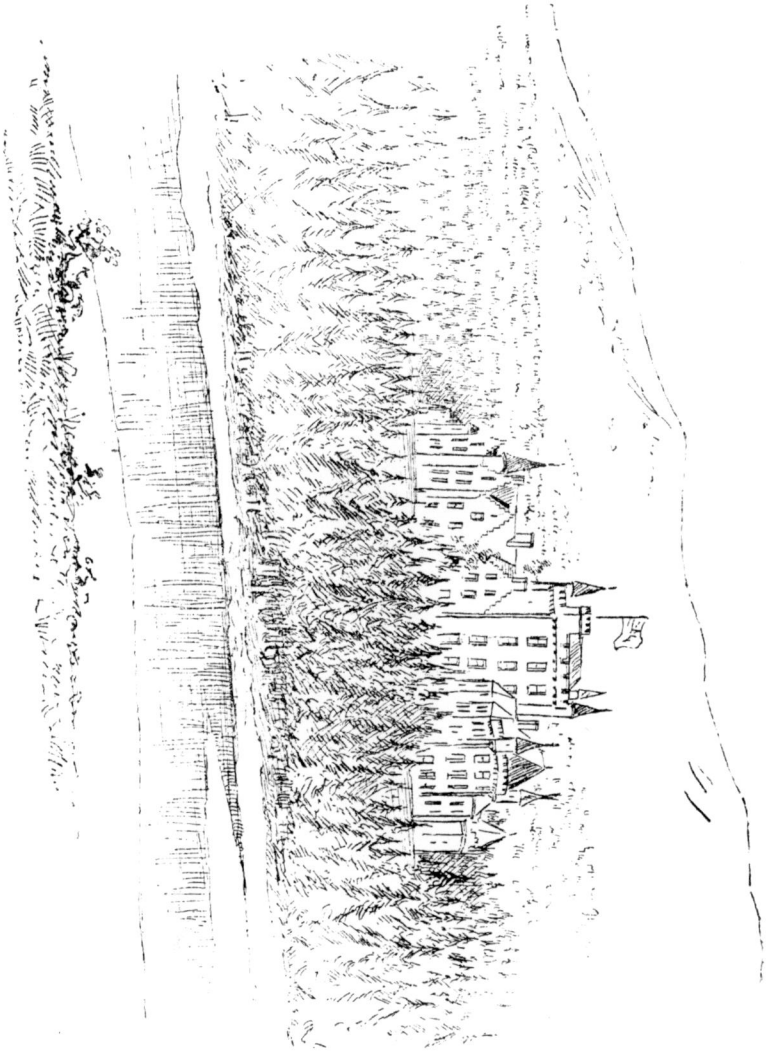

INVERCAULD HOUSE.

over the Falls of the Garbh Allt, while above them ascends Lochnagar with its storm-scarred peaks. On the North-West Ben a' Bhuird rears its mighty form, its corrie'd side showing the gashes and fissures resulting from long-continued warring with natural forces. Altogether it is a scene of mingled sweetness and wildness, of verdure and bareness, of beauty and grandeur scarcely surpassed in Scotland.

The chieftain of the Farquharson clan in 1715, John Farquharson of Invercauld, was a leader, unwillingly enough, in the rising of that year. But the then all-powerful Earl of Mar involved him in the action of the Jacobites, and appointed him to a post of honour in their army. The Highland adherents of the old dynasty met in Invercauld House to arrange their plans, and from that mansion, for nearly the last time in Scotland, the "fiery cross" was sent forth through the hills and glens. In 1745 the same Invercauld chieftain was still alive, but he took no part in the new rising, although the most of the Farquharsons "went out" under the laird of Monaltrie.

Resuming the route to Braemar the traveller has to cross (about 150 yards above the old bridge) the new bridge which was erected at the expense of Prince Albert on the shutting up of the Ballochbuie road. It is a handsome granite structure, known as Invercauld Bridge, and, with the road improvements, cost about £5000. Crossing Invercauld Bridge to the South side of the river the pedestrian will get, as he leans on the Southern parapet, the last peep of Lochnagar obtainable on the journey to Braemar. At the South-West end of the bridge a small burn, the Allt na Claise Moire (the burn of the big hollow), enters the

Dee. There is a "shortcut" along this burn to
Auchallater at the mouth of Glen Callater.

Shortly, after crossing the bridge a big stone may
be observed on the right hand side of the road. It is
known as the "Muckle Stane o' Clunie", and it formed
in olden days one of the landmarks between the pro-
perties of the Erskines of Clunie and the Farquharsons
of Invercauld, but Clunie was long ago swallowed up
in the larger estate. The noted Craig Clunie is on the
opposite (left) side of the road. A recess (a little-beyond
the 56th mile-stone) in this crag, about a third of the
way up, and rather difficult of access, is still known as
the "Charter Chest", from the Invercauld titles and
papers having been concealed there in the troublous
times after the '15. Tradition has it that the laird
himself hid then in the cave there for some months,
and had more than once the mortification of hearing
the Government troops making merry about Invercauld. Soon after passing Craig Clunie the Lion's
Face, another tree-clothed crag, is passed on the left
about 56³/₄ miles from Aberdeen. The rocks on the
upper part of the crag were fancied at one time to have
a resemblance to the features of the king of beasts, but
any likeness of that kind has long been unrecognisable
from the growth of the trees. There is a path by the
Lion's Face and Dubh Chlais (black hollow) to
Castleton and Glen Clunie. The hills on the South
side of the Dee, between Invercauld Bridge and Castleton,
including the Lion's Face and Craig Choinnich,
are composed of quartz rock, gneiss, mica-slate, hornblende rock, granite and limestone.

A short distance beyond the Lion's Face is Craig
Choinnich (Kenneth's Craig), so called from Kenneth

II, who, according to tradition, watched the chase from its summit. At its foot on the opposite (the North) side of the road is Braemar Castle, long the

BRAEMAR CASTLE.

property of the Earls of Mar. After the Revolution the then Braemar Castle was garrisoned with Royal troops to keep the country in subjection; but the natives turned upon the soldiers, and compelled their retreat, thereafter burning the Castle. In 1715 the whole of the Mar estates were forfeited. They were afterwards purchased by Lords Dun and Grange, from whom, in 1730, the John Farquharson of Invercauld, already mentioned, bought the Castle and its lands. In 1748 this same Farquharson leased the remains of the Castle to the War Office, with 14 acres of ground, for the space of 99 years, at the yearly rent of £14. The Government then built the present Castle, and it served for many years as barracks for the soldiers stationed there to keep the Highlanders in check. A more peaceful "gathering of the Clans" than that of the '15 or '45 has, for about half a century past, taken place at the Castle, almost every year, under the auspices of the Braemar Royal Highland Society, whose "games" receive Royal and noble patronage. Racing up Craig Choinnich was formerly one of the items in the programme, but was given up at the request of the Queen, after Her Majesty became aware that the great exertion caused serious injury to the competitors.

About a furlong beyond Braemar Castle, a few yards short of the 58th milestone, the tourist will pass, on the right, the churchyard of Braemar. The old name of the church and parish was St. Andrews, which was changed in the time of Malcom Canmore to Kyndrochet (Bridgend). About the close of Queen Mary's reign, when the Earl of Mar became proprietor of the lands in the district, the name of the parish was again changed, this time to Braemar. The old church stood in the burial-ground, and on its site now stands the burial aisle of the Farquharsons of Invercauld. The old Mackenzies of Dalmore (now Old Mar Lodge), the predecessors of the Duke of Fife in this part of the country, have burial ground close to the West end of the aisle. John Farquharson of the '15 is buried in the aisle, and is surrounded by his descendants. One of the tombstones in the churchyard marks the last resting-place of the oldest "rebel" in Scotland, "Peter Grant, sometime farmer in Dubrach, who died at Auchendryne, the 11th of Feb., 1824, aged 110 years".

About half-a-mile further on is the village of

Castleton of Braemar. The first building reached is the Invercauld Arms Hotel, where a historic rock was blasted almost out of existence some years ago, to allow for an extension of the hotel premises. On that rock on 6th September, 1715, John Erskine, the 39th Earl of Mar, amid a great gathering of clansmen, planted the standard of the Chevalier de St. George, whom he had previously at Glenlivat proclaimed King, by the title of James VIII.

The village of Braemar has grown up on both sides of the Clunie, a tributary of the Dee from the South. The portion on the right bank of the stream is distinguished as Castleton, and is on the Invercauld Estate, while that on the other side is called Auchendryne, and belongs to the Duke of Fife.

In the first quarter of the present century the village was one of the meanest of Highland clachans. It then consisted of a number of low smoky thatched cottages, which, overgrown with grass and noisome weeds, were scattered in all directions without the slightest attempt at regularity. There was then but one inn, and, according to Mr. Grierson, it "was more suitable for drovers and excise officers than any higher description of travellers". On the return of that mountaineering divine to Braemar in 1850 all this was changed, and the village had become a fashionable health resort. But even at that later date Mr. Grierson remarked that certain of the old cottages were "of the olden school, much resembling Irish hovels". Only one or two houses of that class are now to be seen.

Unlike the village of Ballater, the village of Castleton of Braemar is of great antiquity. Under the name of Kyndrochet it was in the olden time long the abode of Royalty and of the nobles who delighted in being near the King. Kenneth II. had here a hunting seat, all trace of which has long disappeared; but the ruins of Malcolm Canmore's Castle are still to be seen at the East end of the bridge over the Clunie. In later days the Bruce was a fugitive in the district for a considerable time, and at a more modern period the Earls of Mar - some of whom scorned to think themselves of lesser dignity than the King on the throne - held high revelry in Braemar. The village is now the fashionable capital of the Deeside Highlands, and is resorted to by health and pleasure seekers from all parts of the kingdom - it might be said of the globe. The summer climate of Braemar is one of the healthiest and most bracing in the British Isles. From the mountaineer's point of view it is a capital centre from which to explore the great Deeside hills - from Lochnagar on the East to the Cairngorms on the West.

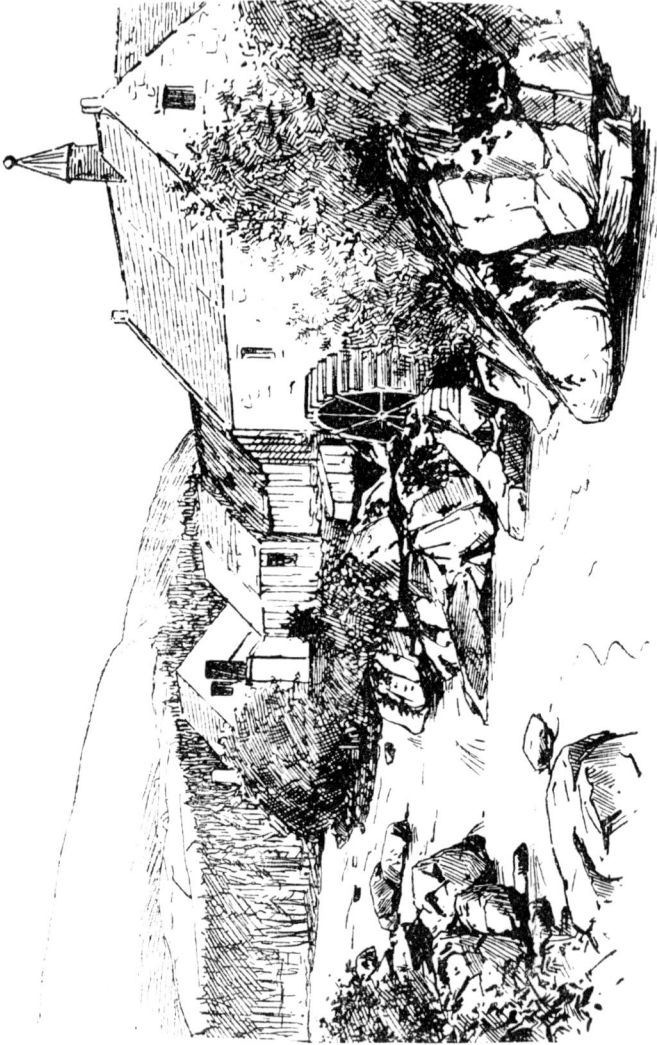

MILL ON THE CLUNIE, BRAEMAR.

# CHAPTER IV.

## BRAEMAR TO LOCHNAGAR.

*I. Castleton to Loch Callater.*

Hail ! Hail ! to the land where the clouds love to rest
Like the shroud of the dead on the mountain's cold breast;
To the cataract's roar where the eagles reply,
And the loch its lone bosom expands to the sky.

BRAEMAR is the most fashionable, as Ballater is
the most popular, point from which to commence the
ascent of Lochnagar. The distance from Castleton to
Cac Carn Beag is about 12 miles, a mile-and-a-half
less than from Ballater, but of the dozen miles from Braemar only 5 can be driven (to Loch Callater Lodge, a
keeper's house), as against 9 when the ascent is made
from the East. The mountain pony is, however, often
called into requisition from the lower end of Loch
Callater.

Leaving Braemar for Lochnagar, the route lies
Southward by Glen Clunie for two miles; then South-
Eastward through Glen Callater to the lower end of
Loch Callater for three miles; and afterwards by a
path in an Easterly direction to the summit. Glen
Clunie is drained by the Water of Clunie, which rises
on the borders of Aberdeenshire and Perthshire, near
the Cairnwell, and joins the Dee a short distance below
the village of Braemar, after a course of about 12 miles.
The Clunie is a capital stream both for trout and
salmon; it belongs almost entirely to the Invercauld
estate. The Duke of Fife, the only other proprietor,

owns the Western bank of the Clunie for about a mile
from its junction with the Dee. The road up Glen
Clunie is on the East side of the stream, and proceeds
by the Cairnwell and Spital of Glenshee to Blairgowrie,
and thence to Dunkeld. Tourists from the South
frequently use this route, which for the most part is
rather wild and picturesque, and is preferred by some
because it saves a long journey going round by Aberdeen.
A four-in-hand coach regularly runs along it each way
during several months in the season. It may be noted
here that Braemar is approachable on wheels only from
the South and the East. There are driving roads West-
wards from Braemar to the Linn of Dee, and to several
shooting lodges in the forest of Mar, but they are not
continuous with carriage roads from the Atholl Valley
or the Speyside district. The approaches to Braemar
from these localities are by mountain paths only.

When leaving Castleton for Lochnagar the traveller's attention is naturally directed at first to two
hills, one on the right (Mor Shron - the big nose), and
the other on the left (Craig Choinnich). The former
has become popularly known as Morrone, and is
composed of quartzose mica-slate with some limestone,
with on the West side dikes of red felspar porphyry.
Morrone rises to a height of 2819 feet above sea level,
and occupies the upper angle formed by the Dee and
the Clunie. The natives maintain that the highest
cultivated land in Scotland is on its North-Eastern
slope, on a ridge called Tomintoul (a by no means
rare name in Gaelic topography), but this statement
has frequently been called in question. It is a pretty
stiff climb to the top of Morrone, but one is well reward-
ed by the "local" views obtained as the ascent is made,

and by the panorama of mountains spread out on all sides around the summit. The mountaineer will be delighted most with the prospect to the North and the North-West. The Cairngorms are visible from the Feshie on the West to the Gairn on the East - such a view of them is had from no other point on Deeside.

Two miles South from Castleton, on the traveller's right, and close to the confluence of the Clunie and the Callater, is the large sheep farm of Auchallater (the field of the wooded stream). The prominent hill immediately to the South, between the Clunie and the Callater, is Sron Dubh (the black nose). Here the Lochnagar tourist leaves Glen Clunie, first crossing the Callater, and then taking the road on the left which leads through Glen Callater. Now, there is not a "reekin' lum" in it, except the keeper's at Loch Callater. The glen has thus rather a desolate aspect, more particularly as it is narrow and bare of trees. The hills are over 2000 feet in height on both sides, and the view is consequently rather confined. The monotony is, however, relieved by the lively burn, which is constantly heard and rarely out of sight, as it brawls and tumbles over its rocky bed, making a series of miniature cascades. The rocks are mostly of mica-slate and granite, mica-slate being quarried at the lower end of the glen for roofing, while limestone occurs at the lower end of Loch Callater. About mid-way between Auchallater and the loch, the burn is crossed by a wooden bridge, which, like the road itself, is much in want of repair. It is understood that any superficial repair the road has received during several years past has been made by the hirers in Braemar, who are not unnaturally interested in preventing it from getting utterly impassable for vehicles. This bridge is a few yards above the junction with the Callater of a short stream, the Allt Coire Ghiubhais, from Loch Phadruig (Peter), a small sheet of water named after a priest, of whom the traveller will hear immediately. The loch itself will be seen as the ascent is made by the path. This priest's name is again met with in Creag Phadruig - an eminence rising to a height of about 2300 feet a little to the South-West of the Loch - and Allt Phadruig, a small burn joining the Callater about half-way between the wooden bridge and the lower end of Loch Callater. Near the bridge is a round-topped green hillock which, in the palmy days of superstition, was accounted a resort of the "little folks". Indeed, Dr. Macgillivray, writing in 1850, says that "on it a man still living has seen fairies dancing, with a piper playing to them". The usual legend crops up here. On a certain Christmas evening two men proceeding from Loch Callater to Castleton heard beautiful music, and saw the little folks dancing on the hillock. One of the men fled precipitately, but the other stayed to feast his ears and eyes, and Christmas came round again before he was discovered as he had been left - standing, admiring the antics of the fairies. At first he declined to leave, as he "hadna been there but for an hour or twa", but he was ultimately rescued from the fascinations of the "green-clad folk".

Loch Callater, 1627 feet above the sea level, is 80 acres in extent and very deep in some parts, the water being black-looking and tinged with peat. Its length is about seven furlongs, and it has a breadth of about

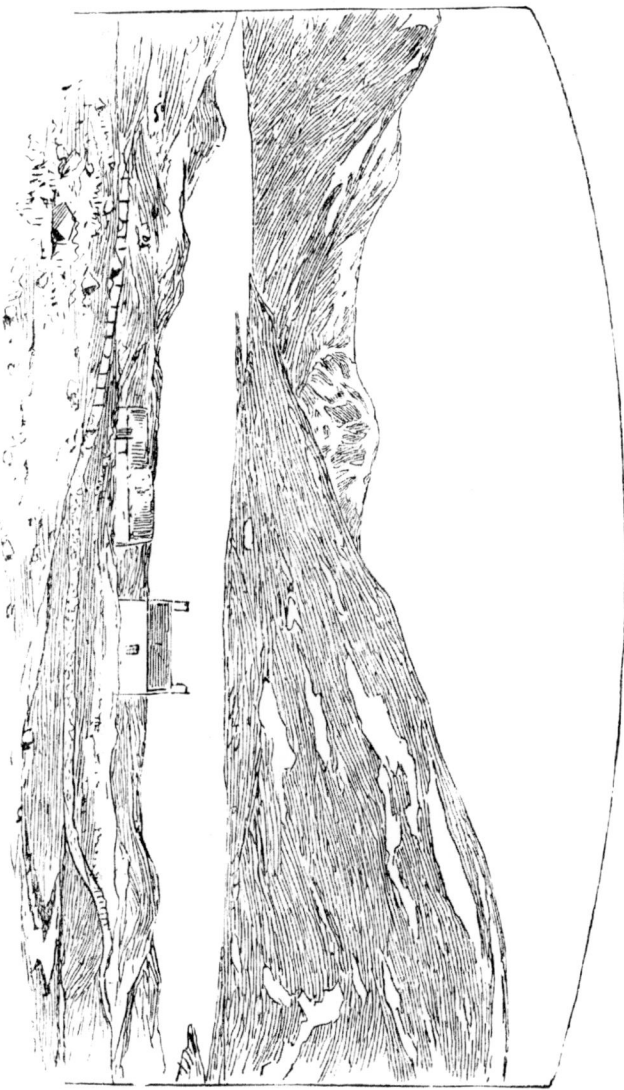

LOCH CALLATER.

one furlong. The loch is a rather tame, treeless, un-
interesting sheet of water, but the upper end is re-
deemed by a grassy haugh, and by the steep rocky
mountains, sharpish peaked, which seem to shut it in.
The *Statistical Account* says that the loch produces
"fine little salmon of about seven or eight pounds
weight and some eel". Salmon are now found up to
fourteen pounds in weight, but they can only be caught
by the net. Trout and large pike are also plentiful.
The neighbourhood of the loch had in former times
a fair population, as is evidenced by the ruins of houses
yet to be seen at both ends, and also by the "larachs"
of shielings about a mile above the head of the
loch. Highlanders   in  former  times  were  always
careful to utilise a flat grassy bit of ground, whether by
a loch or along a burnside.

The principal feeder of Loch Callater is Allt an
Loch (the burn of the loch), which enters at the South-
East end, where the ground is flat and marshy. Allt
an Loch drains the Aberdeenshire side of the mountains that here border on Forfarshire. Along that burn
and over the Tolmount (a mountain which tops the
glen), lies the famous route by Jock's Road to Glen
Doll. As this picturesque "highway" is not yet too
well known - at least at the Callater end - it may not
be out of place to indicate such general directions as
should suffice for the ordinary pedestrian, who wishes
to visit one of the finest glens that a landowner ever
tried to shut up (happily without success). While at
the lower end of Loch Callater, Tolmount (some four
miles distant) will be readily recognised by its "saddle"
- a depression in the ridge to the East of the summit.
This "saddle" has to be made for - first up Loch

Callater, keeping the water on the right, and then ascending by the side of the burn, an intermittent path occasionally assisting the tourist. About three-quarters of an hour's stiff climb will be required for the ascent of the "saddle" itself, and then, bearing a little to the left, a deer fence will be faced. Crossing this fence the track will be struck a little below. Soon Loch Esk, one of the sources of the South Esk, will be seen. The path keeps to the right for Glen Doll, and through it to Glen Clova. The distance between Braemar and Milton of Clova is about 20 miles. An average "time table", based on fairly easy walking, with due allowance for halts, luncheon, &c., may be given as follows:- Braemar to Loch Callater (keeper's house), one-and-a-half hours; to track on summit of Tolmount, two-and-a-half hours; to Jock's Road, one-and-a-half hours; to lower end of Glen Doll, one-and-a-half hours; to Milton of Clova, one hour; total, eight hours.

This digression has led away from Loch Callater, several surroundings of which may properly receive a little more notice. A short path, beginning a few yards East of the keeper's house, leads to a particularly large boulder by the loch side at which is "the Priest's Well", a small chalybeate spring joining the loch. Of course this well has a story associated with it. According to legend, Braemar, at some remote period, suffered from a frost of longer duration and greater strength than even that wintry district had ever previously experienced. The month of May came, but so hard was the ground that not a plough could enter it. Famine being feared, appeal was made to Phadruig, the priest already alluded to. The good man led his anxious flock to this well, which, being of unusual character, was then esteemed of saintly origin. Like all others in the neighbourhood, however, its waters were fast sealed up, but after repeated prayers the well began to thaw. The first water drawn from it was applied to holy purposes. Mass celebrated, the priest resumed his supplications with the gratifying result that the thaw became general. The mountain on which the lowering clouds, intimating the advent of rain, were first seen, was called Carn an t-Sagairt, the Priest's Mountain, but in these degenerate days the name has been corrupted to the more common-place, if not euphonious, form of "Cairn Taggart". Another version of the tradition has it that both priest and people went to Carn an t-Sagairt and remained there until the desired thaw set in. Until a comparatively recent period the Priest's Well - like many of its kind - had considerable popularity, and the usual offerings of coins, buttons, and "preens" were thrown into it.

Another tradition in connection with Loch Callater, and the virtues of a well within two miles of its borders, may not unfitly be narrated here. Sometime about the middle of the seventeenth century there lived in Castleton one Allan M'Hardy, who held the honour-able position of arrow-maker to the Earl of Mar. M'Hardy married, in middle age, a young girl of the district, of more beauty than principle, who seems to have accepted him for his position. Previous to his marriage, Allan had never suffered from a day's illness, but a year or two after it he was seized by an unaccount-able languor and wasting, which local skill and remedies failed to arrest. At last he took counsel with a hermit who lived in the recesses of Aberarder. The hermit directed M'Hardy to proceed to Cairn Taggart, and to drink of a spring he would find there and be cured. The hermit further told him that if at any future time he should be severely stricken in battle, his wound would be immediately healed if it were washed with the water of that well. M'Hardy followed the hermit's advice, and finding himself cured of his illness resolved to leave Castleton and take up his abode at Loch Callater, where he would be within comparatively easy reach of the spring. For some ten years M'Hardy had no occasion to put the water to the test, but at the end of that period he received what seemed certain to prove a mortal wound in a clan fight with the Shaws of Rothiemurchus. At his own request he was carried home, and his first instructions to his wife were that she should bring him water from the well on the Priest's Mountain. As the story runs, the young wife had not been over-grateful to the Aberarder hermit for his previous cure of her husband, and she now resolved to take her own course. She therefore contented herself with drawing water from the Allt a' Chlaiginn (the burn of the skull), which enters the Allt an Loch near the head of Loch Callater. This water had no sooner touched her husband's wound than, uttering the cry "Accursed woman!" he fell back dead. Thereafter the spring on Cairn Taggart received the name of "the arrow-maker's well". It may readily be observed on the Southern slope of the mountain a few yards above the left side of the path, at a height of fully 3000 feet. One of the eminences which rise above the head of the loch, and which still retains the name of Creag an

Fhir-shaighde or Creag an Leisdhair (the arrow-maker's craig), attaining a height of 2800 feet, is believed to have derived its name from M'Hardy's residence at Loch Callater.

Still another story - one even more tragic in its character than that of the arrow-maker - is connected with Loch Callater by the residence there, about the beginning of last century, of a shepherd named William Cameron. He had made his way to Braemar from the country of Lochiel, and had his house on the banks of the Allt a' Chlaiginn at the head of Loch Callater. Cameron was a handsome, brawny fellow, upwards of six feet in height, and in trials of skill and strength had repeatedly shown his superiority over the natives of the district. Further, he had won the love of Elasaid Gordon, whose beauty was famed in every glen in Upper Deeside. Elasaid was the only child of an old shepherd who lived at the Glasallt Shiel, near the head of Loch Muick, and many were the wooers who had sought to gain her favour before she yielded her heart to William Cameron. Among his rivals perhaps the chief was Ian Farquharson, who had proved himself no mean antagonist in Highland sports, and who had also seemed likely to gain the fair Elasaid before Cameron's arrival. Ian had consequently a special grudge against the stranger, alike for his success in the field of "war" and in the court of love, and his envious thoughts regarding Cameron were shared by several companions. The Lochaber man heeded them not, for he was the accepted bridegroom of the flower of Glen Muick, and he was happy. The marriage day was at hand. Willie was paying his last visit to his sweetheart before he should come to be united to her in wedlock, and naturally enough he stayed late. Elasaid Gordon's father, who was regarded as possessed of the second sight, urged him not to leave for Loch Callater that night, warning him - "I see a red mist on the Dubh Loch, and the croak of the raven is in my ears". Cameron laughed at old Alasdair's warning, reassured his betrothed that he would be perfectly safe, as he knew every foot of the way alike in storm and sun, and took a loving farewell. He had need of his knowledge for just as he reached the "Stullan" Burn, about a mile from the shepherd's cottage, a storm of wind and sleet came down with such violence that Cameron was fain to take shelter in the "black" bothy, well known to every man in the glens. There, Ian Farquharson and Rob and Donald Macintosh were hard at work. The smugglers gave Cameron a hearty welcome, and the usquebagh was freely circulated, both in friendship and in anticipation of the approaching happy event. When the storm cleared a little Cameron insisted on going home, and his hosts, whose passions had shown signs of being roused against him, hesitatingly allowed him to depart. Soon, however, they gave chase, and Cameron was overtaken nearly half-a-mile above the Dubh Loch - about two miles from the bothy. The three men there set upon him with their dirks, Farquharson offering him his life if he would give up Elasaid. Cameron refused to purchase life at such a price, and fell by the burnside pierced to the heart, but not before he had inflicted a mortal wound on Farquharson. The Macintoshes carried Cameron's body into a corrie on the South side of the burn, between the Dubh Loch and

Cairn Bannoch, and concealed it in the moss. The snow storm, which had been impending, came down with such persistence that all traces of the murderous struggle were speedily effaced, and, as the Macintoshes kept silence, Cameron's disappearance remained a mystery, although the death of Farquharson gave rise to certain suspicions. Donald Macintosh met his death by violence in a distant part of the Highlands several years afterwards, but before he expired he confessed his share in the crime, and the search thereupon made led to the recovery of Cameron's body. Elasaid Gordon did not long survive the disappearance of her lover, and, with her father, was buried in Glenmuick churchyard, under one of the nameless, rough, coffin-shaped slabs near the Western dyke of the burial-ground. Cameron's remains were interred near the same spot. This story of love and jealousy is now little known, even amongst the oldest inhabitants of the district, but the name of the place where the body was found resulted from the events narrated, and is marked in the Ordnance Survey maps as Coire Uilleim Mhoir (Meikle Willie's Corrie).

---

### BEANNACHD LEAT.

*(A translation from the Gaelic; believed to have been written of Glen Callater, in the beginning of the present century.)*

The long Atlantic waves are saying "Farewell"!
And the winds from the corrie are sighing "Farewell"!
And the burn where the speckled brown trout are dancing is
    calling "Farewell"!
And my heart, my heart is weeping "Farewell"!

Oh ! never, never looked the glen so fair,
Or the wind-beat loch, or the dark moor, or the cliffs where the
     eagles are screaming,
For the round white moon is piercing the mist on the hill -
But not the mist on my heart,
On my heart that is weeping "Farewell, Farewell"!

The white sails are spread for the West,
And the sailors are chanting a merry song as they pull at the
     ropes,
But my heart's song is sad,
And the sails of my desire are not for the West,
And my heart, my heart is weeping "Farewell"!

The sharp keel is slipping through the sea,
And the long shore and the fields and the hills are growing dim,
And my eyes are dim with tears for the land of the heather,
And my heart is weeping, is weeping "Farewell"!

# CHAPTER IV. - *(Concluded.)*

## BRAEMAR TO LOCHNAGAR.

*2. Loch Callater to Cac Carn Beag.*

Now to the mountain's peak,
Whence hills in glory spread,
Hasten, O nature's child!

THE real ascent of Lochnagar begins a few yards short of the keeper's house at Loch Callater, and probably the pedestrian will not be disinclined to exchange the rough stony road along the glen for a mountain path. The track first leads up, and then along, the face of Creag an Loch, a steep ridge that overlooks Loch Callater on its North-East side. Here, however, there is no path such as is described on the Eastern side of Lochnagar. The path is simply a track - at times somewhat indistinct, and in some places marred rather than improved by the ponies that are not infrequently used by tourists. But no real difficulty will be experienced in finding the way by it to Cac Carn Beag. After going along the Southern face of Creag an Loch for about a mile the path takes for nearly another mile a North-Easterly course, and then (at first in a South-Easterly direction) rounds Cairn Taggart at a height of about 3100 feet - about 300 feet below the summit of that mountain.

The view to the South as one proceeds from Creag an Loch to Cairn Taggart is very fine. Loch Callater, immediately below, gets included in a wider view, and loses something of its bleak appearance. Nestling in the Eastern shoulder of Carn an Tuirc (the Boar's Cairn), a mountain rising to a height of 3340 feet, the sheet of water, named on the map Loch Ceann-mor - the "lonely, lonely, dark Loch Candor" of Professor Blackie - charms the eye, about a-mile-and-a-half to the South of Loch Callater. It is situated in a magnificent corrie, at a height of 2196 feet above sea-level, with, according to Dr. Macgillivray, rocks 800 feet high of micaceous slaty quartz, red felspar porphyry, and hornblende slate and rock. Loch Ceann-mor, according to some authorities, refers to Malcolm Canmore and his residence in Braemar. It covers an area of six acres, and contains trout, which have been described as "lean and hungry fishes". The tributary stream to Allt an Loch, rushing headlong down from it, well deserves the name by which it is now known, "the Breakneck Fall", a translation from the Gaelic; "the foxes' stone" - another translated term - is assigned to a particularly large block beside the Breakneck Fall. Loch Candor corrie is famed among botanists all over the country, for the great number of species of Alpine plants it contains. A well-known botanical authority writes of it that it is remarkable for its "rare and characteristic plants, which of themselves would make an herbarium valuable, particularly the *Carex vahlii*, two tufts of which, at least, the situation of which I would not show you, have yet escaped the avaricious eyes and ruthless hands of vagabond botanical vandals".

So steep are the precipices of the corrie of Loch Candor and the Breakneck Fall that occasionally some of the sheep which pasture Glen Callater get into positions from which they have to be rescued by a shepherd let down by a rope. Some thirty years ago a gentleman had a narrow escape from perishing among these rocks. Admiral Jones, while temporarily residing at Braemar, went on a botanical and geological excursion up to Loch Candor. Making a slip on the face of a precipice, he got into a position from which he was unable to release himself. His geological hammer had providentially got wedged so tightly among the stones that it gave him a grip for his hands, and thus enabled him to maintain his footing. During part of three days and two nights it required considerable effort on the part of the Admiral to keep himself from falling headlong down the rocks. Luckily he had directed his servant to meet him at the keeper's house at Loch Callater in the afternoon, and when night came with no appearance of his master, the man gave the alarm at Braemar. A large number of the villagers set out in search as speedily as possible, and one of their parties succeeded in effecting the rescue of the exhausted scientist. The searchers refused all recompense, but Admiral Jones showed his gratitude in gifts to the poor of the district.

Rounding Cairn Taggart, the mountaineer will observe, at the distance of about a mile to the South-South-East, the peak of Cairn Bannoch, which rises to an altitude of 3314 feet, on the borders of the Counties of Aberdeen and Forfar. The principal head stream of the South Esk has its source a quarter-of-a-mile to the West of the peak, while the same distance East, between Cairn Bannoch and the Dubh Loch, is Meikle Willie's Corrie.

From the East side of Meikle Cairn Taggart, the track keeps a more direct course towards Cac Carn

Mor along the Southern slope of flat-topped Little Cairn Taggart. The Dubh Loch will be observed on the right as Meikle Cairn Taggart is rounded, Recently a sheep fence was put up here with a gate where it crosses the path. Near the gate (on the East side of the fence) will be observed a wooden hut, which was placed there in connection with the erection of the fence. The peculiar appearance of this hut will attract attention, but it is easily explained - it was one of the shelter huts used by the British troops in the Crimea, several of which were brought to Invercauld by the late proprietor. It stands at a height of about 3050 feet.

Between the two Cairn Taggarts the path, crosses two small burns (about a quarter-of-a-mile apart), which may properly be regarded as the sources of the Muick. The larger and more Easterly of these burns is the Allt na Da Chraobh Bheath (the burn of the two birch trees). This stream was so called from two birches that grew upon its banks. Near them, according to tradition, a Mowat of Abergeldie overtook two Perthshire caterans on their way South with some of his cattle, which they had "lifted". The reivers were summarily dealt with. The trees were "convanient" as an Irishman would say, and the strangers were soon pendent from their branches.

The routes to Lochnagar from the South naturally converge about the Allt na Da Chraobh Bheath. A few words may now be given about them, so as to indicate how the tourist who wishes to strike out a path for himself, and who does not feel it necessary to restrict himself to the shortest walking route, may reach the summit of Lochnagar. From Glen Clova (not taking into account the Capel Mounth route

which has already been mentioned), the mountaineer
may proceed up the South Esk by Bachnagairn to
Cairn Bannoch, from which the Loch Callater track is
about a mile-and-a-half distant. Preferably, the South
Esk may be left at Bachnagairn, whence a path leads
Northwards to Broad Cairn and Loch Muick. On
leaving the main stream of the Esk at Braedownie,
where it is joined by the White Water, the pedestrian
may go up Glen Doll till he reaches a point on Tolmount near the source of the White Water (the stream
flowing through the glen), and then keep on the ridge
Northwards towards Cairn Bannoch. The route by
Glen Prosen requires that Mayar (a mountain 3043
feet in height at the head of that glen) should be
placed on the left, and when the watershed is thus
reached a Northerly course will be steered to Cairn
Bannoch. From Alyth a way can be found along Glen
Isla and Canness Glen to Tolmount. From the vicinity
of the Cairnwell, Glas Maol (a mountain 3502 feet in
height at the junction of the three Counties - Aberdeen,
Perth, and Forfar) should be made for. Glas Maol is
about a mile-and-a-half East of the road at Cairnwell,
and the route from that mountain lies along the watershed in a North-Easterly direction to Cairn Bannoch
by Tolmount.

From the Allt na Da Chraobh Bheath an ascent of
about 400 feet leads to the plateau of the White
Mount. Coire Lochan an Eoin will be passed on the
left, but a short halt may well be made to inspect what
is the largest corrie on Lochnagar. It is almost as
interesting as its companion on the East, from which it
is about a mile-and-a-half distant. It has three lochans
(one comparatively large, and two small) within its

crags, and there is another fully half-a-mile to the North, at the mouth of the corrie. In the Ordnance Survey maps the latter lochan and the large one within the corrie are misnamed. Lochan an Eoin is the name of the large lochan within the corrie (marked Dubh Loch in the O.S. maps). Its two small neighbours lying to the West are named respectively Lochan na Feadaige (the lochlet of plovers) and Lochan an Tarmachan (the lochlet of ptarmigan) - these birds being common on Lochnagar. The loch at the mouth of the corrie is named the Sandy Loch, probably from the fine sand on its banks, but in the O.S. maps it is erroneously marked "Lochan an Eoin". Stuc Lochan an Eoin is the name of the highest part of the rocks that overtop the lochan a little to the South-West. The "Stuc" divides the corrie into two parts, Lochan an Eoin occupying the Eastern division, and Lochans Feadaige and Tarmachan the Western. Lochan an Eoin lies at a height of 2950 feet, and covers an area of 18 acres; the Sandy Loch is about 350 feet lower, and covers about 15 acres. There are no trout in either of these lochs, which are drained by the Garbh Allt. On the South side of the corrie, North of the path, is the Cairn of Corbreach (the cairn of the speckled corrie), sometimes in old publications referred to as the Quarry of Corbreach. It is extremely likely, however, that the proper name is Cairn of Corbroc (the cairn of the badger corrie). Badgers did at one time abound on Lochnagar, and even yet their footprints are occasionally seen. Carn a' Choire Bhoidheach rises on the South side of the path, opposite Cairn of Corbreach - but neither is distinguished by a "cairn".

"Lochan an Eoin" means the lochlet of birds, and

has probably been so named from the sea-gulls that formerly frequented its banks. Some have erroneously supposed that the name was derived from the eagle. Eagles certainly had at one time eyries on Lochnagar - as already observed, one of the crags by the Dubh Loch derives its name from the king of birds - but now not one has a habitation on the mountain. Eagles have not, however, entirely forsaken the range, for no fewer than five were recently observed together over the summit. A short time ago a couple bred on a tree near Abergeldie Castle, and two of the young birds were taken to Balmoral Castle, near which they are now housed. They are noble-looking birds, and need not a little attention, as a considerable amount of game has to be provided for them. Their voracity may be judged from the fact that they can dispose of a hind in three weeks.

Cairngorm stones were at one time frequently found on Lochnagar, the best crystals being discovered near Lochan an Eoin. The search for such stones was even regarded as a considerable local industry. A writer in 1836 says that he met with parties of "topaz-diggers" in search of the topaz, beryl, and rock-crystal. The Statistical Account says that "what is remarkable, amethysts only are to be found on Lochnagar". A small rent was paid the landowner for the liberty of searching - as was done about the same period on the Cairngorm mountains. Considerable sums are believed to have been made by these "diggers". Cairngorms are now very scarce on Lochnagar, hardly any being found on the surface of the mountain. On the East side of the road near Moine Bad nan Cabar (the mossy thicket of trees), in the upper part of Glen Gelder, lies the "Meikle Stane o' Badachabait", below which, metal, even more precious than Cairngorm stones in their best days, was firmly believed to be hidden. More than one of the natives, acting on the popular belief, have dug for the gold the fairies have concealed there, but without success. They had failed to take the precaution of propitiating the "little green folk", and the fays did not allow their treasures to be molested.

Allt Lochan an Eoin flows through the Sandy Loch in a North-Easterly direction. This stream has a tributary on its right bank called the Black Shiel Burn, from a shepherd's shiel that occupied a site near its source. Between these burns lies Meall na Tionail, a name signifying "the gathering hill". This refers back to the time when Lochnagar was pastured by sheep. When the flocks were collected at the end of the season a general meeting place was appointed for both sheep and shepherds, and animals that had strayed were restored to their respective flocks, as is yearly done yet in several hilly districts. Cattle were grazed on Lochnagar as late as 1877 by a Glen Muick farmer, whose lease entitled him to that right. On Meall na Tionail is a "knap" called "Cnap Nathaireachin" (the adder's knap). From this it may be inferred that adders were formerly more numerous on Lochnagar than they are now. Their scarcity has resulted from the regular burning of the heather, which is thereby prevented from growing to any great height, and consequently affords less shelter than formerly. In a recent season, however, an adder measuring over four feet in length was observed among the heather. White heather, by the way, is rather scarce on the summit and by the paths on Lochnagar, but it is fairly plentiful in localities that obviously need not be pointed out here.

Resuming the track to the summit from Lochan an Eoin, in a little over half-a-mile the tourist will have the source of the Glas Allt close to his right. In this neighbourhood, at a height of from 3250 to 3500 feet above sea level, fir tree roots are to be found. The ancient Caledonian Forest, which occupied the greater part of the North of Scotland, stretched across all the Grampian range of mountains, including Lochnagar. In the beginning of the century the timber grown in Braemar was famed for its excellent quality. This was occasioned by its slow growth, on account of the barrenness of the soil and the elevated situation.

While the mountaineer has the source of a burn noted for its "falls" on the right (the Glas Allt), there are on the left the sources of the Garbh Allt, a burn equally remarkable for its cascades. The highest source of the Garbh Allt is a spring a few yards South-West of Cac Carn Beag, which peak has been for sometime prominently in the view of the mountaineer. The spring will be found very conveniently situated for the thirsty traveller, and with a very little labour an excellent well could be formed. It is not generally distinguished by a particular name, but the name "Poacher's Well", which the writer heard given to it a good many years ago, appears not altogether unsuitable. It is told that in the last decade of the eighteenth century, two poachers, cousins, were out on the White Mounth after ptarmigan in Christmas week. The younger man accidentally fell and broke his leg in the neighbourhood of the Cac Carns. His cousin left him by this well till he should get assistance from the vicinity of Balmoral, but by the time help arrived a heavy fall of snow had smothered the helpless poacher. Shooting ptarmigan and grouse was a favourite form of poaching on Lochnagar, and was much engaged in by the natives of the glens, mainly from a natural love of sport. When the Earl of Aboyne, the head of the Gordon family, parted with Abergeldie, including a considerable portion of Lochnagar, he retained the right of occasionally shooting on the White Mounth. This right was mostly used in the ptarmigan season, and was naturally rather inconvenient for the Balmoral and Abergeldie estates when the Prince Consort came into occupation, and accordingly, it is understood, the Marquis of Huntly's right on Lochnagar was bought up.

From the source of the Glas Allt the path to the summit rises in a North-Easterly direction about 300 feet, after which the mountaineer will find himself at Cac Carn Mor, a quarter-of-a-mile to the North of which is Cac Carn Beag. This is said to be a comparatively modern name for the highest point of Lochnagar, the ancient name being, stated to be "Tacheern", a word indicating the point where "two lairds' lands meet".

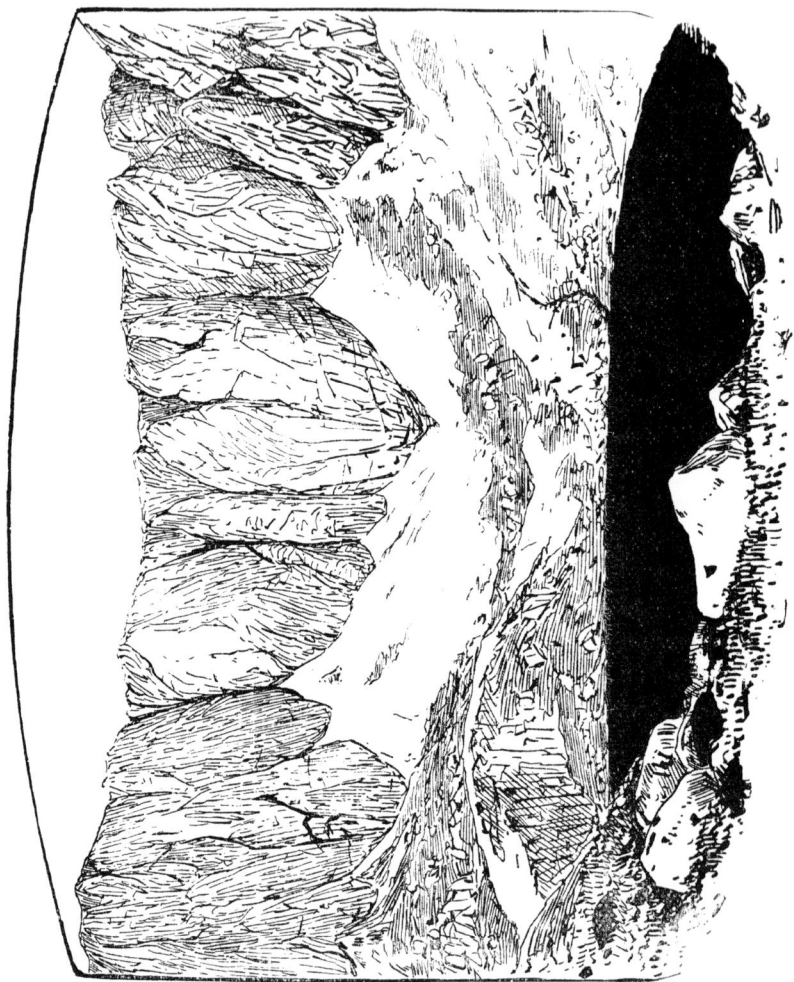

"THE STEEP FROWNING GLORIES OF DARK LOCHNAGAR"

# CHAPTER V.

## ON LOCHNAGAR.

Ye crags and peaks, . . .
How high you lift your heads into the sky,
How huge you are, how mighty and how free!

THE mountaineer who has reached the summit of Lochnagar will now naturally wish to learn what is to be seen from the highest points of the mountain. The weather is often fickle at such heights, even when a cloudless day might be expected; but let it be presumed that the climber has been fortunate, and that the atmosphere is clear. Under these conditions the prospect from the top of Lochnagar is wide and pleasant. The extent of the view to the sea horizon from the Cac Cairns is about 80 miles; but hill-tops may be seen to a greater distance according to their elevation above sea level and the state of the atmosphere.

The tourist will probably first betake himself to Cac Carn Beag, the natural pinnacle-like top that has so long towered above him from whatever side of the mountain the ascent has been made. There, one is almost exactly at the centre of the mountainous mass which has become known as Lochnagar. The Mither Tap (though not the highest point) of Bennachie bears pretty much the same relation at a distance to the mountain of the Garioch as does the Cac Cairn Beag to Lochnagar. Standing on the rock which forms the culminating point, and looking Dee-wards (to the

North), the summit of the mountain sinks in an undulating line along the West side of Glen Gelder
towards Balmoral Castle and the river. The Castle
itself is not seen, Craig Gowan intercepting the view.
To the right is *the* loch (Lochnagar), hemmed in on
the East side by the Meikle Pap, which, although over
3000 feet in height, has now sunk into comparative
insignificance. Beyond Meikle Pap is the Conachcraig range and the glen of the Muick. To the left
(still facing the Dee) is the other great Corrie of
Lochnagar, Coire Lochan an Eoin, with its three
lochlets. The line of the streams that converge from
this corrie leads the eye over the Falls of Garbh Allt,
in the direction of Invercauld, while more to the West
of the corrie are Cairn Taggart and Glen Callater.
Turning right round, facing the South, the mountaineer
has the elevated tableland of the White Mounth
immediately in front. It is drained on the South side
by the Dubh Loch and the Glas Allt, the loch
separating peaked Cairn Bannoch and the very
appropriately named Broad Cairn from the mountain
on which the tourist has taken his stand. Cuidhe
Crom and the Little Pap will now be on the left, to
the South of the Meikle Pap.

Having thus briefly noticed the immediate surroundings, so as to enable the mountaineer who has
made the ascent for the first time to understand
his position, the writer may direct attention to the
more distant views. These extend from beyond the
Moray Firth on the North to beyond the Firth of
Forth on the South, and from the German Ocean on
the East almost to the Atlantic on the West. On
this point there can be no better authority than that

observant mountaineer Dr. Macgillivray, who, writing in 1850, said:- "From it [Cac Carn Beag], as well as from some other parts of the summit, is obtained a most extensive view of the country around, as far as the Lothians, Stirlingshire, the Southern Grampians, many of the Perthshire mountains, those of the upper extremity of Aberdeenshire, beyond them some of the great prominences of the Counties of Argyle and Inverness; ridges and hills even beyond the Moray Firth, as well as the lower Eastern tracts, extending from thence to Aberdeen, and onwards to the Lammermuirs. The mountains of the adjoining part of Forfarshire were much lower, less rugged, and more verdant. The Grampians from Aberdeen to Dunkeld appeared to form a continuous range, broader to the West of Lochnagar, and not affected by the apparently insignificant valley of the Dee. . . Viewed from this peak, the greater part of the country seems mountains".

The first ascent, of which particular record remains, was that made in 1810 by the agriculturalist-parson, the Rev. George Skene Keith, D.D., minister of Keithhall and Kinkell. In addition to writing on agriculture - on which subject he was an authority - he was a mighty climber of mountains, and a measurer of their altitude. It says not a little for his accuracy as a mountain-surveyor that he found the height of the highest peak of Lochnagar - which by the way he calls Ca Cuirn - to be "almost exactly 3800 feet", a difference of only about 14 feet from that obtained by the Royal Engineers with all their costly modern scientific instruments. He made a stay of three hours on the summit, enjoying a capital view. The party had scrambled up "the Ladder" without incident, but in the descent several awkward tumbles were made, the spirit level being lost, and one gentleman rolling down nearly a hundred feet. The reverend gentleman "felt a considerable inflammation in the pleura from the great rains and exertions of yesterday", and accordingly he considered it judicious to lose about eight ounces of blood!

Mr. Grierson was also fortunate in his view from the summit in 1852. He distinctly saw Ben Nevis and Ben Cruachan to the South-West, Schiehallion, Ben Lawers, Ben More, the Ochils, the Lomonds, and the Pentlands over Ben Arti, close to West Lomond to the South. He saw also the Sidlaw Hills, the sea at St. Andrews, Montrose, Aberdeen, and the mouth of the Moray Firth, Bennachie, Ben Rinnes, and all the nearer mountains, with the most of Deeside.

The lighthouse on the Island of May has, according to keepers, been seen from Cac Carn Beag with the naked eye. The following mountains within a radius of 28 miles are also among those seen from the summit - the situation being given only of such of them as have not been already particularly mentioned:- Mayar (Glen Doll), Beinn a' Ghlo (Glen Tilt), Broad Cairn, Mount Blair (between Shee Water and River Isla), Glas Maol (between Cairnwell and Canlochan), Tolmount, Ben Iutharn Bheag (Glen Ey), An Sgarsoch (Glen Geldie), Morrone, Beinn Bhrotain (on the South side of Glen Geusachan), Ben Muich Dhui, Cairngorm, Beinn a' Bhuird, Ben Avon, Meall na Gaineimh, Culardoch, Brown Cow (near head of Strathdon), Corryhabbie (Glen Fiddich), Buck of Cabrach (near head of Deveron), Morven, Mount

Keen, Kerloch (Glen Dye), and Mount Battock (between Glen Dye and Glen Esk).

The far-famed loch, with its encircling precipices, is, of course, the principal attraction in the vicinity of the summit. The upper parts of the crags are to be seen at considerable distances, and in many places the precipices are steep enough to send a shudder through almost any mountaineer, so that the tourist, whose head is not absolutely free from "lightness", should never venture too near the edge. The loch lies at a height of 2575 feet above sea level, and covers an area of 32 acres, the crags above standing at from about 3500 to 3700 feet above sea level. The precipices seem, in some cases, ready to hurl down their rocky pinnacles into the loch below. Indeed, some of these pinnacles have the appearance of being built up artificially of loose blocks, and look

> As if an infant's touch could urge
> Their headlong passage down the verge.

There are several fissures known as "spouts", between the precipices, which may be descended with comparative safety. "The Red Spout" is to the South of the loch and may be descended by a party; but the "Black Spout" (which may have been observed from Glen Muick), nearer Cac Carn Beag, will only admit of one person at a time, because if there were two, the second man could not avoid inadvertently dislodging stones that must fall upon the first. The descent to the loch can, however, be easily and safely made from Cac Carn Beag by keeping the crags well on the right. On reaching the lower end of the loch, the ascent may be

made up the Meikle Pap, towards the beaten path.
The loch swarms with trout of a very fair size, but
they are generally stiffish to take, unless a slight
breeze agitates the water. Permission to fish is of
course necessary. The trout are so numerous that at
times the surface of the loch has the appearance of
"boiling" with them. They were first placed there
in 1851. Snow is generally found in the gullies above
the loch till late in the season. As recorded in the
*Edinburgh New Philosophical Journal* for 1830, some
gentlemen on a geological excursion found here, in
the month of August, a mass of snow, 30 yards square
and several feet deep, from its appearance evidently
a year or two old, the interior being granular like the
ice of glaciers.

The Queen's first ascent of Lochnagar was made
on 16th September, 1848, by the Ballochbuie Forest
and the "Smuggler's Shank". The excursion turned out
to be by no means of the pleasant nature of Her
Majesty's later ascents, and indeed had rather a
disagreeable termination. A brief account of it is
given in *Leaves*:- "We went through that beautiful
wood [Ballochbuie] for about a mile, and then turned
and began to ascend gradually, the view getting finer
and finer; no road, but not bad ground-moss,
heather, and stones . . . . The view of Beinn
a' Bhuird, and indeed of all around, was very beautiful;
but as we rose higher we saw mist over Lochnagar
. . . . It became cold and misty when we were
on Lochnagar . . . . It was quite soft, easy
walking, and we looked down on two small lochs
called Lochan an Eoin, which were very striking,
being so high in the hills  . . .   The ascent com-

menced, and with it a very thick fog, and when we had nearly reached the top of Lochnagar the mist drifted in thick clouds so as to hide everything not within a hundred yards of us. Near the peak . . . we got off and walked, and climbed up some steep stones to a place where we found a seat in a little nook, and had some luncheon. But, alas! nothing whatever to be seen; and it was cold and wet and cheerless. At about twenty minutes after two we set off on our way downwards, the wind blowing a hurricane, and the mist being like rain, and everything quite dark with it. When we had gone on about an hour-and-a-half the fog disappeared like magic, and all was sunshine below - about 1000 feet from the top, I should say. Most provoking! and yet one felt happy to see sunshine and daylight again". A side-light is thrown on this account by an anonymous writer in *Tait's Magazine* the following year. He states that the morning of this ascent of the Queen's was particularly fine, although it was the day following that upon which himself and others were nearly storm-staid on the summit. In the course of the forenoon of the day on which Her Majesty made the ascent the mist came down very thick on the hills, and after noon a heavy drizzling rain began to fall in the glens. Considerable anxiety was felt at Balmoral Castle for the Royal party. The Queen had been expected back by about one o'clock, but did not reach the Castle till after six. There can be no doubt, says this writer, that Royalty was literally lost on Lochnagar for part of a very disagreeable day, the guides, having according to his statement, lost their way in the thick mist.

It may thus be seen that even under the most

auspicious circumstances Lochnagar will at times cause
trouble and inconvenience to its worshippers. And
this notwithstanding the fact already mentioned that
there is a track across the mountain from Glen
Muick on the East to Glen Callater  on the    West.
There is no path, however, between the Cac Cairns -
Cac Carn Beag lying about a quarter-of-a-mile to the
North  of the track - and  this  slight deficiency has
been  enough  at times to  lead  the unwary  astray.
More  than  once  the  writer  has  seen parties, on
descending, thoughtlessly making for the Braemar, in
place of the Ballater track, or proceeding towards the
source of the Glas Allt, under the impression that they
were going directly towards Alltnaguibhsaich Lodge.
The surest way for strangers is to return from Cac
Carn Beag to Cac Carn Mor near where the Braemar
and Ballater tracks meet, and then make a careful
start for their destination. A cairn just below Cac
Carn Mor guides tourists crossing from the East to
the West, or *vice versa*, the cairn being in line with
what may be described as the through route over
Lochnagar. The way once thoroughly lost on a
mountainous mass it  is useless to wander backwards
and forwards, upwards and downwards, in search of
the track; the only course left, short of remaining out
on the spot till daybreak - and that is generally to be
deprecated - is to keep by the first burn that is touched
on and follow it till a house, or other sure indication
of the neighbourhood, is reached. A compass, a
good map, and, if possible, an aneroid should be
carried;  and with  ordinary carefulness all  risk  is
reduced to a minimum, and the mountains become
safer than the crowded streets of a city.

Even experienced hillmen, however, have lost their way on Lochnagar; reference need only be made to a party that, a year or two ago, had to spend a cheerless night in the open. A start was again made in the early morning, but it was not till after several hours walking that the belated mountaineers found that they were proceeding along the South Esk! A not unusual hallucination had seized the wanderers at an early hour the previous evening - they fancied that their compass had gone wrong, and that the needle was pointing Southwards!

Lochnagar has, moreover, claimed more than one life. Just to the North of the loch, on the South-East of Meall Coire na Saobhaide (the corrie hill of the foxes' den), is the Coire na Saobhaide. Between the latter and Cac Carn Beag a man fell down a shelving rock some half-dozen years ago and was killed. He was engaged at Balmoral as a joiner, and had made an excursion to Lochnagar with several companions. He had let his knife slip down the rocks, and in trying to recover it lost his life. About thirty years ago a man threw himself over the precipice above the loch, and was of course killed. A clergyman met his death a few years ago near Loch Callater; but his was a case of exhaustion following on a weak state of health. On the "Smuggler's Shank" there is a stone (visible from Cac Carn Beag) erected to the memory of a gentleman who died there while out from Invercauld grouse-shooting. He drank of water near by when heated, and did not rise again. The inscription runs:-

*IN MEMORY OF*
*GEORGE HOUSTON ESQ[R].  YOUNGER*
*OF*
*JOHNSTONE CASTLE*
*Who Died on this spot while out Shooting*
*14[th.] September 1843*

———— ✳ ————

*Take ye heed, Watch and Pray: for*
*ye know not when the time is.*
MARK XIII, 33  Verse

About 1830 a party of country folks made the ascent of Lochnagar by Loch Muick and Lochan Buidhe. The party included a Tarland farmer, who, by some means or other, fell over the crags at the summit and was killed. An article in *Tait's Magazine* (1849) says:- "The glance downwards to the deep, dark tarn at the bottom of these stupendous rocks is terrific. With a high wind blowing from the West, or a light head, it is dangerous. An over-anxious curiosity has proved fatal in more than one instance. Not very long ago, an individual in a pleasure party, buoyant in spirits, and trusting to a sure foot and a steady eye, in utter defiance of remonstrances by the guides, went too near the edge, lost his balance, and was destroyed".

About three miles East of Ballater, on the South side of the Dee, is the farm of Ballaterach, near where the Pollagach Burn enters the Dee. Here Lord Byron spent some of the early years of his life, the recollection of which, according to his own statement, gave birth to his stanzas on Lochnagar (quoted below).

He alludes, in the fourth stanza, to his "maternal ancestors, 'the Gordons', many of whom fought for the unfortunate Prince Charles, better known by the name of the Pretender. This branch was nearly allied by blood, as well as attachment, to the Stewarts. George, the second Earl of Huntly, married the Princess Annabella Stewart, daughter of James the First of Scotland. By her he left four sons: the third, Sir William Gordon, I have the honour to claim as one of my progenitors". The young poet's wooden "box-bed" was shewn at Ballaterach until a few years ago, when it was accidentally burned.

## LOCHNAGAR.

Away, ye gay landscapes, ye gardens of roses!
  In you let the minions of luxury rove;
Restore me the rocks, where the snow-flake reposes,
  Though still they are sacred to freedom and love:
Yet, Caledonia, beloved are thy mountains,
  Round their white summits though elements war;
Though cataracts foam 'stead of smooth-flowing fountains,
  I sigh for the valley of dark Lochnagar.

Ah! there my young footsteps in infancy wander'd;
  My cap was the bonnet, my cloak was the plaid;
On chieftains long perish'd my memory ponder'd,
  As daily I strode through the pine-cover'd glade.
I sought not my home till the day's dying glory
  Gave place to the rays of the bright polar star;
For fancy was cheer'd by traditional story,
  Disclosed by the natives of dark Lochnagar.

"Shades of the dead! have I not heard your voices
  Rise on the night-rolling breath of the gale"?
Surely the soul of the hero rejoices,
  And rides on the wind, o'er his own Highland vale.

Round Lochnagar while the stormy mist gathers,
  Winter presides in his cold icy car:
Clouds there encircle the forms of my fathers;
  They dwell in the tempests of dark Lochnagar.

"Ill-starr'd, though brave, did no visions foreboding
  Tell you that fate had forsaken your cause"?
Ah! were you destined to die at Culloden,
  Victory crown'd not your fall with applause:
Still were you happy in death's earthy slumber,
  You rest with your clan in the caves of Braemar;
The pibroch resounds, to the piper's loud number,
  Your deeds on the echoes of dark Lochnagar.

Years have rolled on, Lochnagar, since I left you,
  Years must elapse ere I tread you again:
Nature of verdure and flow'rs has bereft you,
  Yet still are you dearer than Albion's plain.
England! thy beauties are tame and domestic
  To one who has roved o'er the mountains afar:
Oh for the crags that are wild and majestic!
  The steep frowning glories of dark Lochnagar!

----

THE Author desires to express his acknowledgments to the Proprietors of the *People's Journal* for the use of the Zinco-blocks for the illustrations given in the preceding pages. "Lochnagar" appeared in serial form in that paper during the summer of 1891, but has been considerably extended and carefully revised for this volume.

## CHAPTER VI.

## ITS GEOLOGY AND BOTANY.

The adamantine rock, the fragile flower,
The equal work of an Almighty power.

## GEOLOGY.

*(Communicated.)*

LOCHNAGAR, with the hills and lower tracts of country immediately around it, consists of granite, which is continued on the range of hills on the South side of the Dee for about 30 miles to the East. This granite tract in Braemar is flanked on the North, the West, and the South by other rocks, such as gneiss, mica-slate, quartzite, limestone, &c.; and some of these rocks intervene between the two granite tracts of Lochnagar and the Cairngorms.

The following paragraphs have been compiled from the authorities quoted, and from the facts given much can be learned, in studying carefully the superficial rock phenomena of Lochnagar and vicinity, of the principles of geology, physical and chemical.

According to Professor W. Macgillivray, LL.D. (in his *Natural History of Deeside and Braemar*, a work printed in 1855 soon after his death, by command of the Queen, for private circulation, and to which we have more than once had occasion to refer), Lochnagar rises majestically above all other mountains on the South side of the Dee, and has more dignity than any other Scottish mountain except Ben Nevis. Along with its projections and dependencies, some extending miles into the surrounding tract, it consists of granite, rather coarse-grained, reddish, with, a little mica. The felspar is pale flesh-coloured, in irregular concretions or imperfect crystals; the quartz, dark brownish grey; and the mica, brownish black, in very small scales. The granite is similar to that composing the Cairngorm or Monadh Ruadh (red) mountains. The rock is easily frangible, and has decomposed very extensively in the abrupt crags of the corries of the mountain. In the great precipice the fissures of the rock are nearly vertical, with transverse rents, giving the appearance of stratification; while the rude parallel horizontal joints of the weathered rock look like cyclopean masonry. It is only in the upper ruin-like parts that the rock is thus split into tabular fragments or plates. Further down it is more distinctly fissured, and on the unbroken surface of the upper part of the mountain it is solid and massive. The aspect of the precipice viewed from the base of its talus near the lake is singular and most imposing, the rock being fissured by perpendicular chasms, and having a vast accumulation of enormous blocks near the base.

Some of the tremendous granite precipices, says Mr. T. F. Jamieson, F.G.S. (in the *Quarterly Journal of the Geological Society*, 1860), so common in the Central Highlands of Braemar, and mostly on the Eastern flanks of the higher mountains, as in the case of Lochnagar, rear a vertical front of 1000 or even 1500 feet above their base, which is often 2200 or 2500 feet above the sea. The rocks and corries of these Highland mountains remind one of the ironbound coast so well depicted by Professor Forbes in

"Norway and its Glaciers". They resemble ancient sea cliffs in a sea full of floating icebergs.

Lochnagar (says Sir Archibald Geikie, Director-General of the Geological Survey of the United Kingdom, in his Scenery of Scotland, 1887) shows how frost splits solid rocks into separate blocks, and how it disintegrates their surface by the freezing of water between their particles. The grim precipice, nearly a mile long, and 300 to 500 feet in vertical depth, yawns below as we look from the crest of the mountain N.N.E. into the valley of the Dee. There, sheltered from the sun, the snow lingers long into the summer, and frost finds its congenial home. Inch by inch the vertical joints of the granite of the precipice are being opened further into the face of the cliff. Along the edge can be seen the process in all its stages, the fine rift just starting like a crack in a window pane up to the loose pillar, now standing gaunt and alone in front awaiting its eventful hurl into the gulf below. Far down between the base of the precipice and the little tarn, which lies gleaming in the shade of the mountain, can be seen the grey slopes, encumbered with *debris*, which appear from the height of the spectator mere trails of sand, but they are really avalanches of granite blocks, many of them hundreds of tons in weight, now travelling slowly to the plains, still a prey to rain and frost, sun and storm, and slowly breaking up into loose fragments as they descend.

Portions of the felspar of the granite *debris*, by the action of air and water containing oxygen and carbonic acid, are decomposed. The alkali in the mineral is dissolved out, leaving a powdery substance

called kaolin, the basis of clay, and composed of
silicate of alumina. The more indestructible quartz
grains fall apart to form the coarse sand on the hill,
the grains being about the size of swan shot No. 1.,
partridge shot, and sparrow hail. The quartz particles,
with those of the felspar, which resist chemical action,
will in time, by attrition in running water, be reduced
to fine sand grains in their course down the Dee, and
be finally washed ashore on the Aberdeen beach, and
blown inland by the wind on the already existing
sand dunes along the coast.

The top of Lochnagar (continues Sir Archibald
Geikie) at a level of 3500 feet above the sea, is one
of those remarkable flat-topped moorlands which, in
the Eastern Grampians, rise to 3000-4000 feet above
the sea. It is a broad undulating moorland upwards
of a mile-and-a-half long, gently sloping Southward to
Loch Muick, and ending in the North at the edge of a
range of granite precipices, at the base of which is one
of those moraine tarns, or small sheets of water like
those around the Cairngorm mountains, which have
been ponded back by some of the vast masses of
angular rubbish disengaged by frost and ordinary
atmospheric waste from cliffs, crags, and steep slopes,
falling on glaciers, and sped by them as they melted
away in their final disappearance. Such tarns occur
in hundreds in the Scottish Highlands, generally at
the head of the glens or at the mouths of corries.

According to Mr. Lionel Hinxman, B.A., of the
Geological Survey of Scotland, an interesting feature
connected with Lochnagar is the stream of moraines
issuing from the great corrie, and flowing over the
lesser hills down into Glen Muick at Birkhall.

# BOTANY.

## THE FLOWERING PLANTS AND FERNS OF LOCHNAGAR,

### AS DEFINED IN THIS WORK.

*By John Roy, LL.D., Aberdeen.*

*(The Species are arranged under their Classes and Natural Orders.)*

#### CLASS. I.-DICOTYLEDONOUS OR EXOGENOUS FLOWERING PLANTS.

Ranunculaceae -

*Thalictrum alpinum*, L., Alpine Meadow Rue.

*Anemone nemorosa*, L., Wood Anemone.

*Ranunculus peltatus*, Fr., Water Crowfoot.

*R. heterophyllus*, Sibth., Water Crowfoot.

*R. hederaceus*, L., Ivy Crowfoot.

*R. Flammula*, L,, Small Spearwort.

*R auricomus*, L., Wood Crowfoot.

*R. acris*, L., Upright Meadow Crowfoot, Butter-
    cup,

*R. repens*, L., Creeping Crowfoot.

*Caltha palustris*, L., Common Marsh Marigold.

*Trollius Europaeus*, L., Mountain Globe-Flower.

*Aquilegia vulgaris*, L., Common Columbine.

Fumariaceae -

*Fumaria officinalis*, L., Common Fumitory.

Cruciferae -

*Arabis petraea*, De Cand., Alpine Rock Cress.

*A. hirsuta*, Br., Hairy Rock Cress.

*Cardamine pratensis*, L., Common Bitter Cress,
    Ladies' Smock, Cuckoo-flower.

*C. hirsuta*, L., Hairy Bitter Cress.

*Nasturtium officinale*, Br., Common Water Cress.

*Cochlearia officinalis*, L., Common Scurvy Grass.

*Draba verna*, L., Common Whitlow Grass.

*Teesdalia nudicaulis*, Br., Naked Stalked Teesdalia.

*Sisymbrium Thalianum*, Hooker, Thale Hedge Mustard.

*Subularia aquatica*, L., Water Awl-Wort. Rare.

*Capsella Bursa Pastoris*, De Cand., Common Shepherd's Purse.

*Lepidium Smithii*, Hooker, Mithridate Pepper Wort.

*Sinapis arvensis*, L., Charlock Mustard.

*Raphanus Raphanistrum*, L.,Wild Radish. Jointed Charlock.

Cistaceae -

*Helianthemum vulgare*, Gaert., Common Rock Rose.

Violaceae -

*Viola palustris*, L., Marsh Violet.

*V. canina*, L. (*V. Riviniana*, Reich.), Dog's Violet.

*V. tricolor*, L., Pansy Violet or Heartsease.

*V. lutea*, Hudson, Yellow Mountain Violet.

Droseraceae -

*Drosera rotundifolia*, L., Round-leaved Sundew.

*D. anglica*, Hudson, Great English Sundew. Rare.

*Parnassia palustris*, L., Common Grass of Parnassus.

Polygalaceae -

*Polygala vulgaris*, L., Common Milkwort.

Elatinaceae -
> *Elatine hexandra,* De Cand., Hexandrous Water-
> wort, Water-pepper.   Very Rare.

Caryophyllaceae -
> *Silene acaulis,* L., Moss Campion, Dwarf Silene.
> *S. inflata,* Smith, Bladder Campion.
> *S. maritima,* With., Sea Campion.
> *Lychnis Flos-cuculi,* L., Ragged Robin, Meadow
> Lychnis.
> *L. diurna,* Sibth., Red Campion.
> *Sagina procumbens,* L., Procumbent Pearl-wort.
> *S. saxatilis,* Wimm., Alpine Pearl-wort.
> *S. subulata,* Wimm., Awl-leaved Pearl-wort.
> *S. nodosa,* L., Knotted Pearl-wort.
> *Arenaria serpyllifolia,* L., Thyme-leaved Sand-
> wort.
> *Stellaria media,* With., Common Chickweed.
> *S. holostea,* L., Greater Stitchwort.
> *S. graminea,* L., Narrow-leaved Stitchwort.
> *S. uliginosa,* Murr., Bog Stitchwort.
> *Cerastium triviale,* Link., Mouse-ear Chickweed.
> *C. glomeratum,* Thuil., Mouse-ear Chickweed.
> *C. alpinum,* L., Hairy Alpine Chickweed.

Paronychiaceae -
> *Spergula arvensis,* L., Corn Spurrey.
> *Spergularia, rubra,* St. Hilaire, Field Spurrey.

Linaceae -
> *Linum catharticum,* L., Purging Flax.

Hypericaceae -
> *Hypericum pulchrum,* L, Small upright St. John's
> Wort
> *H. hirsutum,* L., Hairy St John's Wort.

Geraniaceae -
*Geranium sylvaticum* L., Wood Crane's Bill.
*G. pratense,* L., Blue Meadow Crane's Bill.
*G. Robertianum,* L., Herb Robert.
*G. Molle,* L., Dove's-foot Crane's Bill.
*G. dissectum,* L., Jagged or cut-leaved Crane's Bill.

Oxalidaceae -
*Oxalis Acetosella,* L., Common Wood Sorrel.

Aquifoliaceae -
*Ilex aquifolium,* L., Holly.

Leguminosae -
*Ulex Europoeus,* L., Furze, Whin or Gorse.
*Genista Anglica,* L., Needle Gorse, Petty Whin.
*Spartium scoparium,* L., Common Broom.
*Anthyllis Vulneraria,* L., Common Kidney-vetch.
*Trifolium repens,* L., White Trefoil or Dutch Clover.
*T. pratense,* L., Purple Clover.
*T. medium,* L., Zigzag Clover.
*Lotus corniculatus,* L., Common Bird's-foot Trefoil.
*Vicia sepium,* L., Bush Vetch.
*V. Cracca,* L., Tufted Vetch.
*V. sylvatica,* L., Wood Vetch.
*Lathyrus pratensis,* L., Meadow Vetchling.
*Z. macrorrhizus,* Wimm., Tuberous Vetchling.
*Lupinus perennis,* L., Lupin.

Rosaceae -
*Prunus communis,* Hudson, Common Plum.
*P. Padus,* L., Bird Cherry.
*Spiroea Ulmaria,* L., Meadow-sweet.

*Dryas octopetala,* L., White Dryas.    Rare.

*Geum rivale,* L., Water Avens.

*G. urbanum,* L., Common Avens.    Rare.

*Rubus Idoeus,* L., Common Raspberry.

*R. saxatilis,* L., Stone Bramble.

*R. Chamoemorus,* L., Mountain Bramble or Cloud-berry.

*Fragaria vesca,* L., Wood Strawberry.

*Comarum palustre,* L., Purple Marsh Cinque-foil.

*Potentilla anserina,* L., Silver-weed Cinque-foil.

*P. alpestris, Hal.,* Orange Alpine Cinque-foil.

*P. Tormentilla,* Sibth., Tormentill.

*P. Sibbaldia,* L., Procumbent Cinque-foil.

*Alchemilla vulgaris,* L., Common Lady's Mantle.

*A. alpina,* L., Alpine Lady's Mantle.

*A. arvensis, Sm.,* Field Lady's Mantle.

*Rosa spinosissima,* L., Burnet-leaved Rose.

*R. tomentosa,* Sm., Downy-haired Rose.

*R. villosa,* L., Villous Rose.

*R. mollis,* Sm., Soft Rose.

*R. canina,* L., Dog-Rose, including many so-called varieties.

*Pyrus Aucuparia,* Gaert., Rowan-tree.


Onagraceae -

*Epilobium angustifolium,* L., Rose-bay Willow-herb.

*E. montanum,* L., Mountain Willow-herb.

*E. obscurum,* Schreb., Square-stalked Willow-herb.

*E. palustre,* L., Marsh Willow-herb.

*E. alsinifolium,* L., Chickweed-leaved Willow-herb.

*E. alpinum,* L., Alpine Willow-herb.

Haloragaceae -
*Myriophyllum. alterniflorum*, De Cand., Water-
Milfoil,

Portulaceae -
*Montia fontana*, L., Water Blinks.

Crassulaceae -
*Sedum Rhodiola*, De Cand., Rose-root Stonecrop.
*S. villosum*, L., Hairy Stonecrop.

Saxifragaceae -
*Saxifraga stellaris*, L., Starry Saxifrage.
*S. nivalis*, L., Alpine-clustered Saxifrage.   Rare.
*S. oppositifolia*, L, Purple Mountain Saxifrage.
*S. rivularis*, L., Alpine Brook Saxifrage.   Rare.
*S. aizoides*, L., Yellow Mountain Saxifrage.
*S. hypnoides*, L., Mossy Saxifrage.
*Chrysosplenium oppositifolum*, L., Common
Golden Saxifrage.

Umbelliferae -
*Sanicula Europoea*, L., Wood Sanicle.
*Pimpinella saxifraga*, L., Common Burnet-Saxifrage.
*Bunium flexuosum*, With., Common Earth-nut.
*Meum athamanticum*, Jacq., Bald Money, High-
land Micken.
*Angelica sylvestris*, L., Wild Angelica.
*Heracleum sphondylium*, L., Common Cow-Par-
snip.
*Anthriscus sylvestris*, Koch, Wild Beaked-Parsley.

Cornaceae -
*Cornus suecica*, L., Dwarf Cornel.

Araliaceae -
*Adoxa Moschatellina*, L., Tuberous Moschatell.

Caprifoliaceae -
*Lonicera Periclymenum*, L., Common Honeysuckle
or Woodbine.
*Linnoea borealis*, Gronov, Two-flowered Linnaea.

Rubiaceae -
*Galium verum*, L., Yellow Bed-straw.
*G. saxatile*, L., Smooth Heath Bed-straw.
*G. palustre*, L., White Water Bed-straw.
*G. boreale*, L., Cross-leaved Bed-straw.
*Sherardia arvensis*, L., Blue Field-madder.
*Asperula odorata*, L., Sweet Woodruff.

Valerianaceae -
*Valeriana officinalis*, L., Great wild Valerian.

Dipsaceae -
*Scabiosa succisa*, L., Devil's-bit Scabious.

Compositae -
*Apargia autumnalis*, Willd., Autumnal Hawk-bit.
*Hypochaeris radicata*, L., Long-rooted Cat's-ear.
*Mulgedium alpinum*, Less., Alpine Blue Sow-
Thistle. Very Rare.
*Crepis paludosa*, Moench, Marsh Hawk's Beard.
*Sonchus arvensis*, L, Corn Sow-Thistle.
*Leontodon Taraxacum*, L, Common-Dandelion.
*Hieracium Pilosella*, L., Common Mouse-ear
Hawk-weed.
*H. alpinum*, L., Alpine Hawk-weed.
*H. holosericeum*. Back., Silky Hawk-weed. Rare.
*H. calenduliflorum*, Back., Marigold Hawk-weed. Rare.
*H. nigrescens*, Willd., Black-haired Hawk-weed.
*H. senescens*, Back., Gray Hawk-weed.
*H. chrysanthum*, Back., and var. *micranthum*
Back., Golden-flowered Hawk-weed.

*H. anglicum*, Fr., English Hawk-weed.
*H. Iricum*, Fr., Irish Hawk-weed.
*H. argenteum*, Fr., Silvery Hawk-weed.
*H. murorum*, L., Wall Hawk-weed.
*H. vulgatum*, Fr., Common Hawk-weed.
*H. prenanthoides*, L., Rough-bordered Hawk weed. Rare.

*H. corymbosum*, Fr., Clustered Hawk-weed.
*Lapsana communis*, L., Common Nipple-wort.
*Saussurea alpina*, De Cand., Alpine Saussurea. Rare.

*Carduus crispus*, L., Curled-leaved Thistle. Rare.
*Cnicus lanceolatus*, Willd., Spear Plume Thistle.
*C. palustris*, Willd., Marsh Plume Thistle.
*C. arvensis*, Hoffm., Creeping Plume Thistle.
*C. heterophyllus*, Willd., Melancholy Plume Thistle.

*Centaurea nigra*, L., Black-discoid Knap-weed.
*C. Cyanus*, L., Corn Blue-bottle.
*Artemisia vulgaris*, L., Common Mugwort.
*Antennaria dioica*, Gaert, Mountain Everlasting.
*Gnaphalium sylvaticum*, L., Highland Cudweed.
*G. Norvegicum*, Gunn, Norwegian Cudweed. Very Rare.

*G. supinum*, L., Dwarf Cudweed.
*Filago minima*, Pers., Least Filago.
*Tussilago Farfara*, L., Colt's-foot.
*Solidago Virga aurea*, L., Common Golden-rod.
*Senecio vulgaris*, L., Common Groundsel.
*S. Jacoboea*, L., Common Ragwort.
*S. aquaticus*, Hudson, Marsh Ragwort.
*Bellis perennis*, L., Common Daisy.

*Chrysanthemum Leucanthemum*, L., Great White Ox-eye.

*C segetum*, L., Corn Marigold or Yellow Ox-eye.

*Matricaria inodora*, L., Scentless Feverfew.

*Achilloea millefolium*, L., .Common Yarrow.

*A. Ptarmica*, L,, Sneeze-wort.

Campanulaceae -

*Campanula rotundifolia*, L., Harebell.

Lobeliaceae -

*Lobelia Dortmanna*, L., Water Lobelia.

Vacciniaceae -

*Vaccinium Myrtillus*, L., Blaeberry.

*V. uliginosum*, L., Bog Whortleberry.

*V. Vitis Idoea*, L., Red Whortleberry, Cranberry of this district.

*V. Oxycoccos*, L., Marsh Whortleberry, Cranberry. Rare.

Ericaceae -

*Erica Tetralix*, L., Cross-leaved Heath.

*E. cinerea*, L., Fine-leaved Heath.

*Calluna vulgaris*, Salisb., Common Ling, Heather.

*Loiseleuria procumbens*, Desv., Trailing Azalea.

*Arctostaphylos Uva-ursi*, Sprengel Black Bear-berry.

Pyrolaceae -

*Pyrola secunda*, L., Serrated Winter-green.

*P. rotundifolia*, L., Round-leaved Winter-green. Very rare.

*P. media*, Swartz, Intermediate Winter-green.

*P. minor*, L., Less Winter-green.

Gentianaceae -

*Gentiana campestris*, L., Field Gentian.

*Menyanthes trifoliata*, L,, Buckbean.

Boraginaceae -
*Myosotis repens*, Don, Creeping Water Scorpion-grass.
*M. coespitosa*, Schultz, Tufted Water Scorpion-grass.
*M. arvensis*, Hoffm., Field Scorpion-grass.
*M. versicolor*, Lehm., Yellow and Blue Scorpion-grass.
Scrophulariaceae -
*Veronica serpyllifolia*, L., and var. *humifusa*, Dickson, Thyme-leaved Speedwell.
*V. alpina*, L., Alpine Speedwell. Rare.
*V. scutellata*, L., Marsh Speedwell.
*V. Beccabunga*, L., Brooklime.
*V. officinalis*, L., Common Speedwell.
*V. Chamoedrys*, L., Germander Speedwell.
*V. hederifolia*, L., Ivy-leaved Speedwell.
*V. agrestis*, L., Field Speedwell.
*V. arvensis*, L., Wall Speedwell.
*Euphrasia officinalis*, L., Common Eyebright.
*Rhinanthus Crista-galli*, L., Common Yellow-rattle.
*Melampyrum pratense*, L., Common Yellow Cow-wheat.
*M. sylvaticum*, L., Lesser-flowered Yellow Cow-wheat.
*Pedicularis palustris*, L., Marsh Louse-wort.
*P. sylvatica*, L., Pasture Louse-wort.
*Scrophularia nodosa*, L., Knotted Figwort.
*Digitalis purpurea*, L., Purple Foxglove.
Labiatae -
*Mentha arvensis*, L., Field Mint.
*Thymus Serpyllum*, L., Wild Thyme.

*Teucrium Scorodonia,* L., Wood Germander.
*Ajuga reptans,* L., Common Bugle.
*Galeopsis Tetrahit,* L., Common Hemp-nettle.
*G. versicolor,* Curtis, Large-flowered Hemp-nettle.
*Lamium purpureum,* L., Purple Dead-nettle.
*L. amplexicaule,* L., Henbit-nettle.
*Stachys sylvatica,* L., Wood Woundwort.
*S. palustris,* L., and var. *ambigua,* Marsh Wound-
    wort.
*Nepeta Glechoma,* Benth., Common Ground-Ivy.
*Calamintha Clinopodium,* Benth., Common Wild
    Basil. Rare.
*Prunella vulgaris,* L., Common Self-heal.
Lentibulariaceae -
*Pinguicula vulgaris,* L., Common Butterwort.
*Utricularia vulgaris,* L., Greater Bladderwort.
Primulaceae -
*Primula vulgaris,* Hudson, Common Primrose.
*P. veris,* L., Common Cowslip.
*Trientalis Europoea,* L., European Chickweed
    Winter-green.
*Lysimachia nemorum,* L., Wood Loose-strife.
Plumbaginaceae -
*Armeria maritima,* Willd., Common Sea-pink.
Plantaginaceae -
*Plantago major,* L., Greater Plantain.
*P. lanceolata,* L., Ribwort Plantain.
*P. maritima,* L., Sea-side Plantain.
Chenopodiaceae -
*Chenopodium album,* L., White Goose-foot.
Scleranthaceae -
*Scleranthus annuus,* L., Annual Knawel.

Polygoriaceae -
  *Polygonum viviparum*, L., Viviparous Bistort.
  *P. Aviculare*, L., Common Knot-grass.
  *P. Convolvulus*, L., Climbing Polygonum.
  *P. Persicaria*, L., Spotted Polygonum.
  *Rumex crispus*, L., Curled Dock.
  *R. obtusifolius*, L., Blunt-leaved Dock.
  *R. aquaticus*, L., Grainless Water Dock.
  *R. Acetosa*, L., Common Sorrel.
  *R. Acetosella*, L., Sheep's Sorrel.
  *Oxyria reniformis*, Hooker, Kidney-leaved
    Mountain-Sorrel.
Empetraceae -
  *Empetrum nigrum*, L., Black Crowberry.
Euphorbiaceae -
  *Mercurialise perennis*, L., Perennial or Dog's
    Mercury.
  *Euphorbia Helioscopia*, L., Sun Spurge.
  *E, Peplus*, L., Petty Spurge.
Callitrichaceae -
  *Callitriche stagnalis*, Scop., Starwort.
  *C. verna*, L., Vernal Water Starwort.
  *C. hamulata*, Kg., Starwort.
  *C. autumnalis*, L., Starwort.    Rare.
Urticaceae -
  *Urtica urens*, L., Small Nettle.
  *U. dioica*, L., Common Nettle.
Myricaceae -
  *Myrica Gale*, L., Sweet Gale, Bog Myrtle.
Betulaceae -
  *Betula glutinosa*, Fr., Common Birch.
  *B. nana*, L., Dwarf Birch.   Common between
    2000-3000 feet altitude.

*Alnus glutinosa,* Gaert, Common Alder.

Salicaceae -

*Salix Caprea,* L., Great Round-leaved Willow.

*S. aurita,* L., Round-leaved Willow.

*S. Lapponum,* L., Downy Willow.

*S. repens,* L., Creeping Willow.

*S. nigricans,* Sm., Dark-leaved Willow.

*S. herbacea,* L., Least Willow.

*S. reticulata,* L., Reticulated Willow.    Rare.

*Populus tremula,* L., Trembling Poplar or Aspen.

Cupuliferae -

*Quercus Robur,* L., Common British Oak.

*Corylus Avellana,* L,, Common Hazel.

Coniferae -

*Pinus sylvestris,* L., Scotch Fir.

*Juniperus communis,* L.,and var. *nana,* L.,Common
   Juniper.


CLASS II. - MONOCOTYLEDONOUS OR ENDOGENOUS
FLOWERING PLANTS.

Orchidaceae -

*Malaxis paludosa,* Sw., Bog Orchis.

*Listera ovata,* Br., Common Tway-blade.

*L. Nidus-avis,* Rich., Bird's-nest Orchis.    Very
   Rare.

*L. cordata,* Br., Heart-leaved Tway-blade.

*Goodyera repens,* Br., Creeping Goodyera.

*Orchis maculata,* L., Spotted palmate Orchis.

*Gymnadenia conopsea,* Br., Fragrant Gymnadenia.

*G. albida.* Rich., Whitish Gymnadenia.

*Habenaria viridis,* Br., Green Habenaria.

*H. chlorantha,* Bab., Great Habenaria.

Juncaceae -
*Juncus communis*, Meyen, Common Rush.
*J. triglumis*, L., Three-flowered Rush.
*J. trifidus*, L., Trifid Rush.
*J. acutiflorus*, Ehrh., Sharp-flowered Rush.
*J. lamprocarpus*, Ehrh., Shining-fruited Rush.
*J. nigritellus*, D. Don, Black-headed Rush.
*J. supinus*, Moench., Upward Rush.
*J. squarrosus*, L., Heath Rush.
*J. bufonius*, L., Toad Rush.
*Luzula sylvatica*, Bich., Great Hairy Wood-Rush.
*L. pilosa*, Willd., Broad-leaved Hairy Wood-Rush.
*L. campestris*, Willd., Field Wood-Rush.
*L. multiflora*, Lej., Many-flowered Wood-Rush.
*L. spicata*, De Cand., Spiked mountain Wood-Rush.
*L. arcuata*, Hooker, Curved mountain Wood-Rush.
    Very rare.
*Narthecium ossifragum*, Hudson, Bog-Asphodel.

Juncaginaceae -
*Triglochin palustre*, L., Marsh Arrow-grass.

Typhaceae -
*Sparganium minimum*, Fr., Small Bur-Reed.

Naiadaceae -
*Potamogeton lucens*, L., Shining Pondweed.
*P. heterophyllus*, Schreb., Various-leaved Pond-weed.
*P. natans*, L., Sharp-pointed Broad-leaved Pond-weed.
*P. polygonifolius*, Pourr., Many-angled Pond-weed.

Cyperaceae -
*Schoenus nigricans*, L., Black Bog-rush.

*Rhyncospora alba,* Vahl., White-beak-rush. Very
   rare.
*Eleocharis palustris,* R. Br., Creeping Spike-rush.
*Isolepis setacea,* R. Br., Bristle-stalked Mud-rush.
*Scirpus pauciflorus,* Lightf., Few-flowered Club-
   rush.
*S. coespitosus,* L., Scaly-stalked Club-rush.
*Eriophorum vaginatum,* L., Hare-tail Cotton-
   grass.
*E. angustifolium* Roth., Narrow-leaved Cotton-
   grass.
*Carex dioica,* L., Dioecious Carex or Sedge.
*C. pulicaris,* L., Flea Carex.
*C. pauciflora,* Lightf., Few-flowered Carex.
*C. leporina,* L., Hare's-foot Carex.
*C. helvola,* Blytt, Pale red Carex.   Very rare.
*C. lagopina,* Wahl., Hare's-foot Carex.   Very rare.
*C. canescens,* L., White Carex.
*C. stellulata,* Good., Prickly-headed Carex.
*C. atrata,* L., Black Carex.
*C. vulgaris,* Fr., Common Carex.
*C. rigida,* Good., Rigid Carex.
*C. flava,* L., Yellow Carex.
*C. Oederi,* Ehrh., Oeder's Carex.
*C. fulva,* Good., Tawny Carex.
*C. binervis,* Sm., Green-ribbed Carex.
*C. vaginata,* Tausch., Short brown-spiked Carex.
   Rare.
*C. panicea,* L., Pink-leaved Carex.
*C. pallescens,* L., Pale Carex.
*C. capillaris,* L., Dwarf capillary Carex.
*C. rariflora,* Sm., Loose-flowered Carex.
*C. glauca,* Scop., Glaucous Heath Carex.

*C. proecox*, Jacq., Vernal Carex.

*C. pilulifera*, L., Round-headed Carex.

*C. ampullacea*, Good., Slender-beaked Bottle Carex.

Gramineae -

*Anthoxanthum odoratum*, L., Sweet-scented Vernal-grass.

*Nardus stricta*, L., Common Mat-grass.

*Alopecurus pratensis*, L., Meadow Fox-tail-grass.

*A. alpinus*, Sm., Alpine Fox-tail-grass.   Rare.

*A. geniculatus*, L., Kneed Fox-tail-grass.

*Phleum alpinum*, L., Alpine Cat's-tail-grass.   Very rare.

*Calamagrostis Epigejos*, Roth., Wood Small-reed. Very rare.

*Agrostis vulgaris*. With., Fine Bent-grass.

*Aira coespitosa*, L., Tufted Hair-grass.

*A. alpina*, L., Smooth Alpine Hair-grass.   Very rare.

*A. flexuosa*, L., Waved Hair-grass.

*A. setacea*, Hudson, Bristle-stalked Hair-grass.

*A. caryophyllea*, L., Silvery Hair-grass.

*A. proecox*, L., Early Hair-grass.

*Molinia coerulea*, Moench, Purple Molinia.

*Melica nutans*, L., Mountain Melic-grass.

*Holcus mollis*, L., Creeping Soft-grass.

*H. lanatus*, L., Meadow Soft-grass.

*Koeleria cristata*, Pers., Crested Koeleria.

*Poa fluitans*, Scop., Floating Meadow-grass.

*P. pratensis*, L., Smooth-stalked Meadow-grass.

*P. trivialis*, L., Rough Meadow-grass.

*P. alpina*, L., Alpine Meadow-grass.   Rare.

*P. laxa*, Hoenke, Wavy Meadow-grass.   Very rare.

*P. minor*, Gaud., Smaller Meadow-grass. Very rare.

*P. nemoralis*, L., Wood Meadow-grass.

*P. annua*, L., Annual Meadow-grass.

*Triodia decumbens*, Beauv., Decumbent Heath-grass.

*Briza media*, L., Common Quaking-grass.

*Dactylis glomerata*, L., Rough Cock's-foot-grass.

*Cynosurus cristatus*, L., Crested Dog's-tail-grass.

*Festuca bromoides*, Sm., Barren Fescue-grass.

*F. ovina*, L., Sheep's Fescue-grass.

*Bromus commutatus*, Schrad., Altered Brome-grass.

*B. mollis*, L., Soft Brome-grass.

*Avena pratensis*, L., and var. *alpina*, Sm., Narrow-
leaved Perennial Oat.

*A. elatior*, L., False Oat-grass.

*Triticum repens*, L., Creeping Wheat or Couch-grass.

*Lolium perenne*, L., Perennial or Beardless Rye-
grass.


CLASS III. - ACOTYLEDONOUS OR CELLULAR PLANTS.

Polypodiaceae -

*Polypodium vulgare*, L., Common Polypody.

*P. Phegopteris*, L., Pale Mountain Polypody.
Beech Fern.

*P. Dryopteris*, L., Tender Three-branched Polypody. Oak Fern.

*P. alpestre*, Hoppe, Alpine Polypody. Rare.

*Aspidium Lonchitis*, Sw., Rough Alpine Shield-
fern. Holly Fern. Rare.

*A. Oreopteris,* Sw., Heath Shield-fern.
*A. Filix-mas,* Sw., Blunt Shield-fern. Male Fern.
*A. dilatatum,* Willd., Prickly Shield-fern.
*Cystopteris fragilis* Bernh., Brittle Bladder-fern.
*Asplenium septentrionale,* Hull., Forked Spleen-
  wort. Very rare.
*A. Ruta-muraria,* L., Wall-rue Spleen-wort.
*A. Trichomanes,* L., Common Wall Spleen-wort.
*A. viride,* Hudson, Green lanceolate Spleen-wort.
*A. Adiantum-nigrum,* L., Black-stalked Spleen-wort.
*A. Filix-foemina,* Bernh., Short-fruited Spleen-wort.
  Lady Fern.
*Pteris aquilina,* L., Common Brake-fern.
*Cryptogramme crispa,* Br., Parsley Fern.
*Blechnum boreale,* Sw., Northern Hard-fern.

Ophioglossaceae -
*Botrychium Lunaria,* Sw., Common Moon-wort.

Lycopodiaceae -
*Lycopodium clavatum,* L., Common Club-moss.
*L. annotinum,* L., Interrupted Club-moss. Rare.
*L. selaginoides,* L., Lesser Club-moss.
*L. alpinum,* L., Savin-leaved Club-moss.
*L. Selago,* L., Fir Club-moss.

Marsiliaceae -
*Isoetes lacustris,* L., European Quill-wort.

Equisetaceeae -
*Equisetum pratense,* Ehrh., Meadow Horse-tail.
  Rare.
*E. arvense,* L., Field Horse-tail.
*E. sylvaticum,* L., Branched Wood Horse-tail.
*E. limosum,* L., Smooth Naked Horse-tail.
*E. palustre,* L., Marsh Horse-tail.

# THE CORRIE FLOWER.

*By the Author of "The Rival Giants",*
*"The Key o' Bennachie", &c.*

### I.

THE Lady Anne was good and true,
    And fair as fair could be;
Her face revealed not grief nor care,
    Sweet as a flower was she.

She knew not the River of Woe -
    Oh, sad, and joyless theme!
And to her the Stream of Sorrow
    Was but an empty dream.

Her cheek was like the blush-red rose;
    And on her lips, a smile
Lit up her face, Madonna-like -
    A face all free from guile.

Her eyes, sweet mirrors to her soul,
    Shone clear, like beacons bright;
No mariner in wildest storm .
    Would pray for truer light.

In her ear "the old, old story"
    Of young, unsullied love
Was breathed by one of gentle blood,
    Who fain his troth would prove.

Oh, lithe of form and limb was he,
    An arm both sure and strong;
His sword he'er rusted in its sheath,
    But leaped to right the wrong!

And he has vowed his love is true,
    But she, with doubts and fears,
Ties her silk scarf about his arm,
    And whispers through her tears:

"A flower grows by the Loch so weird,
 In dark, sequestered spot;
A harbinger of faithful love -
 The sweet Forget-me-not.

"At dead of night, be't dark or light,
 Now prove thy love for me, -
Go, pluck it, and I'll meet thee
 By th' Allt na Guibhsaich tree".

"Enough, Sweet, 'tis as good as done,
 I'll pluck the flower for thee;
And, Love, thou'lt come and meet me
 By th' Allt na Guibhsaich tree".

With courtly mien he kissed her hand,
 And raised his plume on high,
"Till midnight, dear," he gaily cried,
 "Till then, my Love-Good-bye".


II.

Within proud Abergeldie's Halls,
 The music throbs and swells;
But none is there to say, "they play
 Two loved ones' fun'ral knells".

The stately minuet is danced,
 With wealth of old-world grace,
And in the throng of gallants gay
 Is many a smiling face.

But Lady Anne is ill at ease,
 Her bosom heaves, and sighs
She fain would stifle move her breast -
 The mist stands in her eyes.

And aye a voice was whispering:
 "I've plucked the flower for thee,
Sweet Love, then come and meet me
 By the Allt na Guibhsaich tree".

She heeds not now the honeyed words
    That flow from courtly lips,
And she withdraws her hand from one
    Who'd kiss its finger-tips.

"Go saddle me a horse", she cries,
    "Through bracken and o'er root,
This night I ride to Lochnagar,
    And climb the hill on foot".

Out on the night so black and grim,
    Is heard the distant sound
Of gathering storm. The moaning wind
    Sobs eerily around.

Yet, 'spite the dark and lowering night,
    On, on through dub and mire
She rides, and pauses not to think,
    But seeks her heart's desire!

But, aye the voice kept whispering:
    "I've plucked the flower for thee,
Sweet Love, now come and meet me
    By th' Allt na Guibhsaich tree".

Soon is she at the trysting tree,
    And hastily dismounts;
While the tardy laggard moments
Impatiently she counts.

"Why does my Love, the brave Sir James,
    *Thus* keep his tryst with me"?
She looks beseechingly to heaven,
    Then bends to kiss the tree.

E'en, while she speaks her thoughts revert
    To that secluded spot,
Where she has told her Love he'll find
    The sweet Forget-me-not.

She thinks she sees the corries grim
    Stand out in frowning pride;
"Great God! he may be dead", she screams,
    "Would I were by his side"!

Then, as she ran to climb the hill,
    From out the sullen North,
The storm that had been gathering,
    Impetuously broke forth.

The lightning flashed from peak to peak,
    The thunder pealing deep;
The wind, with loud and threatening howl,
    Adown the corries steep

Rushed, with a great and mighty noise;
    The rain and blinding sleet
Dashed 'gainst the crags with hissing sound
    In one huge crashing sheet.

Up to the precipice she climbs,
    All panting, wet, and worn;
And peering through the darkness, she
    Seeks traces of the morn.

Now, trembling kneels she on the brink,
    Amid the storm's wild shriek,
Her arms outstretched in mute appeal,
    So child-like and so weak.

"Come back, come back, my Love", she cries,
    "Come back, come back to me";
The wind with mocking laugh replies,
    "He'll ne'er come back to thee".

And, as she kneels in mute despair,
    With cruel, searching flash,
The lightning plays adown the Loch ;
    And, ere the thunder's crash

She sees her faithful Lover stretched,
  Within his hand the flower,
The pale-blue, sad Forget-me-not,
  That's now to be her dower.

She sees him but for an instant -
  For God is ever kind -
Yet, the flash that reveals the Lover
  Has struck the loved one blind !

.    .    .    .    .    .    .

'Tis said, when nights are eerie,
  When wind drives from the North,
A sobbing and a wailing,
  Out on the air break forth;

And a voice is heard to whisper:
  "I've plucked the flower for thee,
Sweet Love, then come and meet me
  By the Allt na Guibhsaich tree".

# INDEX.

Dark figures (thus **104**) denote the page; referring more particularly to the subject.

INDEX 187

Page

Kyndrochet, . . . . . 114,116
Ladder, The, . . . . . 74,76,81
*Lady of the Lake, The* (Scott's), . 56
Laird's Bed, The, . . . . . 47
*Leaves* (The Queen's), . . . 56,150
Linn Wood, The, . . . . . 25,39
Lion's Face, The, . . . . . 112
Little Cairn Taggart, . . . . **20**,136
"  Conachcraig, . . . . 79
"  Pap, . . . . . 19,20,26
Littlejohn's Bridge, . . . 75
Loch Callater, . 119,121,**122**,123,133
"  "  Lodge, . . . . . 119
"  Candor, . . . . . . 134
"  Ceann-mor, . . . . . 134
"  Esk, . . . . . . 67,126
"  Muick, . . . . 49,52,**53**,56,76
"  Phadruig, . . . . . 122
Lochan Buidhe, . . . . . 62
"  an Eoin, . . . . . 138
"  Dubh, . . . . . 79
"  na Feadaige, . . . . 138
"  "  Tarmachan, . . . 138
Lochend, . . . . . . 54
Lochnagar -
Boundaries of, . . . . . 16
Corrie of, . . . . . . **81**,144
Deaths on, . . . . . . 153
Distillery, . . . . . . 94
Extent of, . . . . . . 16
Height of, . . . . . . 18
Illustrations, . . . . . . 8,144
Loch of, . . . . 17,146,**149**
Lost on, . . . . . . 152,153
Meaning of, . . . . . . 17
Routes to -
Ballater, . . . . . . 23
Braemar, . . . . . 23,**119**
Dubh Loch, . . . . . 53
Glen Gelder, . . . . . 77,104
Smuggler's Shank, . . . 106
South, . . . . . 136
Strath Girnock, . . . . 78,86
Situation of, . . . . . . 9,14
Snow on, . . . . . . 14,150
Stanzas on, . . . . . 155
Summits of, . . . . . . 18
Time of ascent, . . . . . 74

Page

View from, . . . . . . 145
Lorne, Marquis of, . . . . 64
"Loupin'-on Stane", . . . . 26
Grant, Peter, . . . . . . 114
Macgillivray, Prof. W., LL.D., .105,122,
134,147,157
M'Hardy, Allan, . . . . . 127
Macintosh, Donald, . . . . 130
"  Rob, . . . . . 130
Mackenzie, Sir Allan, . . . . 25,67
"  " James T., . . . 27,28
Mackenzie, W.A., . . . . . 68
Mackenzies of Dalmore . . . 114
Mackinnon, Prof. D., M.A., . . 18
Mar, Earls of, . . 43,91,111,113-6,127
Marquis of Huntly, . . . . 142
"  " Lorne, . . . . 64
Meall Coire na Saobhaidhe, . . 19,153
"  Dubh, . . . . . 48
"  na Gaineimh, . . . . 77
Meall na Tionail, . . . . . 140
Meikle Cairn Taggart, . . . 20
"  Pap, . . 19,20,31,75,76,79
"  Stane o' Badachabait. . 140
"  Willie's Corrie, . . . **131**,135
Micras, . . . . . . 86
Mill of Sterin, . . . . . 25,**39**,44
"  on the Clunie, . . . . 118
Milton of Clova, . . . . . 126
Mitchell, John, . . . . . 40
Moine Bad nan Cabar, . . . 139
Monaltrie House, . . . . . 103
"  Street, . . . . . 103
Monelpie Moss, . . . . . 57,62
Mor Shron, . . . . . . 120
Morrone, . . . . . . 120
Morven, . . . . . . 81
Mount Keen, . . . . 13,76,77,81
Mounth, The, . . . . . . 9,11
"  The White, . . . . 9
Mowat of Abergeldie, . . . 87,136
Muckle Stane o' Clunie, . . . 112
Muick, Bridge of, . . 25,**36**,37,39
"  Falls of, . . . 25,39,**48**
"  Spital of, . . . 26,**31**,55
"Muir of Drumthwacket", . . 12
"  " Inver, . . . . 105
*Natural History of Deeside and*

THE END.

# BRAEMAR (NEAR BALMORAL)

## THE

# Invercauld Arms Hotel,

*(In connection with the Invercauld Arms Hotel Ballater.)*

## The finest Hotel situation in Scotland.

The grandest scenery and the most bracing mountaim air in the Highlands.

# Posting in all its Branches.

### BY APPOINTMENT

## Posting Master to the Queen,

☞ Coaches during the Season to **Blairgowrie, Dunkeld, and Ballater.**

*Letters and Telegrams punctually atrended to.*

# A. McGREGOR,